**Training
Captive-Bred
Parrots**
TS-242

Photographers and Artists: Delia Berlin, Michael DeFreitas, David Dube, Isabelle Francais, M. Gilroy, Barbara Gould, Frank Nothaft, Robert Pearcy, Ronald R. Smith, Ginny Tata-Phillips.

Distributed in the UNITED STATES to the Pet Trade by T.F.H. Publications, Inc., One T.F.H. Plaza, Neptune City, NJ 07753; distributed in the UNITED STATES to the Bookstore and Library Trade by National Book Network, Inc. 4720 Boston Way, Lanham MD 20706; in CANADA to the Pet Trade by H & L Pet Supplies Inc., 27 Kingston Crescent, Kitchener, Ontario N2B 2T6; Rolf C. Hagen Inc., 3225 Sartelon St. Laurent-Montreal Quebec H4R 1E8; in CANADA to the Book Trade by Vanwell Publishing Ltd., 1 Northrup Crescent, St. Catharines, Ontario L2M 6P5 ; in ENGLAND by T.F.H. Publications, PO Box 15, Waterlooville PO7 6BQ; in AUSTRALIA AND THE SOUTH PACIFIC by T.F.H. (Australia), Pty. Ltd., Box 149, Brookvale 2100 N.S.W., Australia; in NEW ZEALAND by Brooklands Aquarium Ltd. 5 McGiven Drive, New Plymouth, RD1 New Zealand; in Japan by T.F.H. Publications, Japan—Jiro Tsuda, 10-12-3 Ohjidai, Sakura, Chiba 285, Japan; in SOUTH AFRICA by Lopis (Pty) Ltd., P.O. Box 39127, Booysens, 2016, Johannesburg, South Africa. Published by T.F.H. Publications, Inc.
MANUFACTURED IN THE UNITED STATES OF AMERICA
BY T.F.H. PUBLICATIONS, INC.

Training Captive-Bred

PARROTS

DELIA BERLIN

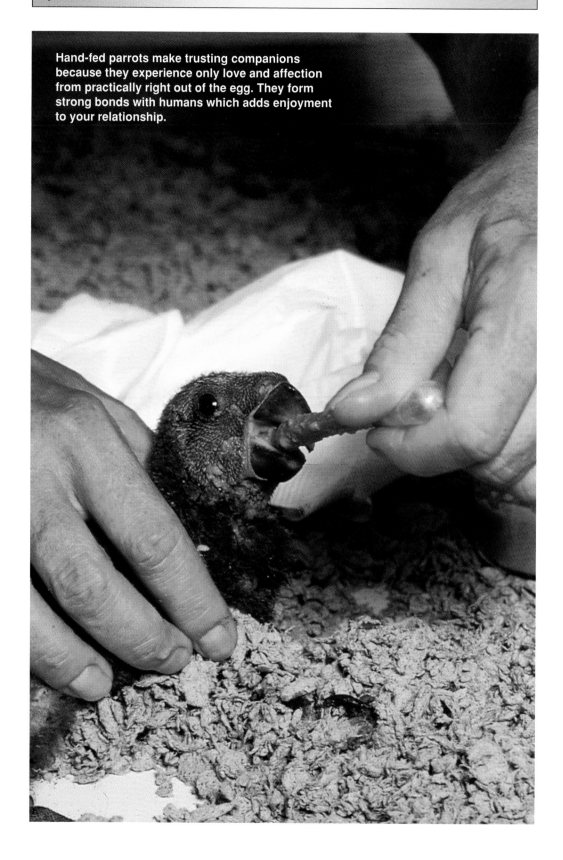

Hand-fed parrots make trusting companions because they experience only love and affection from practically right out of the egg. They form strong bonds with humans which adds enjoyment to your relationship.

Contents

Acknowledgments
6

Foreword
8

Introduction
10

Purchasing Your Baby
14

Preparing for the Arrival
49

The Trip Home
58

Preventing and Detecting Problems
64

Along the Way
86

Epilogue
119

About the Author
120

Index
121

ACKNOWLEDGMENTS

I am specially thankful to Timothee Graze, owner of Featherlust Farms, and Sherry Duhigg, owner of Birds in Brookfield, for their kind and open support and their commitment to responsible parrot breeding. I also thank the Connecticut Association for Aviculture (CAFA) for having provided me with a forum for continuous learning about pet birds and their needs.

In addition, I thank my mother who, albeit begrudgingly, modeled responsible pet keeping by making sure all our animals' cages were cleaned daily, whether her children kept their end of the bargain or not. Also, I thank my husband, my daughter, my sister and my niece, whose humor, enthusiasm and patience helped me finish this book. Last but not least, I thank my parrots, who with the gift of their beauty, joy and affection make me a happy child again, every day.

Delia Berlin

Parrots truly make rewarding pets; they will give back to you every bit of affection that you give to them.

A happy parrot is an irresistible playmate.

Foreword

Imagine yourself at a very young age, surrounded by playful, affectionate peers and cared for by much bigger and powerful creatures. While you don't fear them, you are aware of your differences, and you appreciate their value. They mean food, warmth, clean bedding and safety; they provide for you.

Suddenly, just as you are starting to become a little more independent and adventurous, a little better equipped to play with your peers and to explore your environment, a new group of creatures adopts you. You are separated from your peers and, after a scary trip that you thought would never end, installed in a new housing arrangement.

Everything is different and worrisome. These creatures don't act quite the same; the food is somewhat different; the smells are strange. More than anything, you miss your friends and even your former caretakers, and you wonder what sort of intentions these new ones may have.

After a few days, sadness starts to wane. These caretakers seem good natured, they take real interest in you. You start to feel better about the lack of peers. There is no competition for food or territory, there are no squabbles. And you have enough toys, gadgets and company to stay busy and entertained.

Time flies when you are having fun, and one day you suddenly realize that things have slowly changed. Nobody comes to see you or play with you when you call. The food is not so good anymore. Your quarters don't always get cleaned. The toys are old and have started to bore you. You yearn for something you can't even imagine or understand. You call louder and louder in an effort to be noticed, but this has a negative effect. Sometimes they yell back at you in a scary way; sometimes they put you in the dark; still other times they do both and leave the room. When someone finally comes, you are so frustrated you don't want to play anymore. You bite the first creature that comes near you. That ends the interactions for the day.

After many days of playing different versions of this game, you become depressed and just spend most of your time in a corner, sleeping away. Bad habits, like self-destructive behavior, screaming, pacing and flailing food, fill the rest of your time. Your life may last a day or a century, but you really couldn't care less...

In the proper sensitive household, a pet parrot makes a delightful pet. With good care and respect, parrots can actually thrive in human company.

INTRODUCTION

The preceding story may sound depressing, but it actually gives you a brief imagined experience of what many hand-fed pet parrots go through during their first few years with humans. Some endure circumstances that are far worse, such as verbal and physical abuse, or severe neglect of their most basic needs. Others are sold many times in their lives without any regard for their new environments. Their vocabularies, loaded with curses and reprimands, eloquently tell their stories.

Parrots are intelligent and social creatures. Many learn to talk and to communicate their needs quite well. However, people often misunderstand their potential, leading to disappointment and abuse. A parrot remains a parrot, no matter how smart it seems or how well it can talk. In other words, a parrot's intelligence may lead some to expect much more self-restraint and good manners than the bird is capable of. People easily attribute to parrots meanness and manipulative skills that are merely displacement behaviors, outlets to compensate partially for all they give up to become our companions, or responses to our own callousness.

All parrots are naturally suited for an environment that couldn't be more different from our homes. In becoming pets they give up many pleasures and thrills, such as peer companionship and free flight. They may learn to count, sing and do tricks, but they may not always understand or accept the rules we try to impose on them.

Although this cage is slightly small for this parrot, apparently the owners are concerned for the parrot's well being; the cage is equipped with vertical and horizontal bars, plenty of toys, varied perches and swings and a cage-top perch.

Parrots are naturally suited for an environment that couldn't be more different from our homes. They give up many pleasures and thrills to become our companions.

The more a baby parrot is gently handled, played with, groomed and talked to, the more enjoyable it is. It will, however, grow to depend on this contact that must be provided for the rest of its life.

A good environment for a parrot will provide protection, security, and nourishment.

This is not to say that parrots can't live happy lives as pets. With appropriate care, empathy and respect they can actually thrive in human company. Sensitive humans can make interesting friends. Many humans, however, fall short from sensitive to an animal's needs. It often amazes me how many people ask me if my parrots can talk even after they have been in our home while the parrots were talking. Caged birds seem to be "invisible" to many humans.

A good household provides shelter, protection, nourishment, health care, hygiene and social stimulation. Parrots certainly can't always count on such comfortable lives in the wild. Stress and danger are experienced daily and their life spans are much shorter than in captive conditions. If you get a pet parrot, you should

make up with good care for what your friend is missing in order to keep you company.

This book is intended to help you build a solid foundation for your new relationship. For breeders and pet dealers, this book should facilitate the process of giving you the information necessary to provide a happy home for a bird. Caring for a pet parrot is much like caring for a child that will never outgrow toddlerhood. There will always be good days and bad days. Understanding your pet will help you put things in perspective and prevent, rather than exacerbate problems.

Parrots are like children; they have their good days and their bad. Caring for a pet parrot is much like caring for a child that will never outgrow toddlerhood.

PURCHASING YOUR BABY...

GENERAL CONSIDERATIONS

If you still haven't purchased a hand-fed baby parrot, there are a few things you should consider carefully. The first one is whether you really should have one. If you purchased this book you probably want one, but you may not know what it's going to be like. This is what you need to know before you buy:

Parrots are very long-lived. In the case of some larger parrots their life span in captivity may reach one hundred years. Even small ones tend to live longer than most dogs or cats. Over the years our families are likely to experience moves, births, deaths, marriages, divorces, shifts in job schedules, and many other changes. You should ask yourself if you are likely to sustain enough interest in your pet to maintain social stimulation, to provide support during transitions, and to avoid drastic changes in the

Before acquiring a hand-fed baby, serious thought must be given to what will become of your pet parrot should you, or other members of your household, become ill. This African Grey chick has the potential to live in excess of fifty years.

time and attention you will give to your pet. You should also be aware that you will have to make early efforts to socialize your parrot to be flexible and adaptable in order to

cope with inevitable changes without overwhelming stress.

Parrots form strong, life-long bonds. In the case of hand-fed parrots, these bonds are formed with people. The parrot's family will be its flock. You need to assume responsibility for its social stimulation for a long time. These bonds are not easily transferable. When families are forced to give up a pet parrot for adoption, the bird will not always adapt to its new home. Also because of this, satisfactory boarding and pet-sitting are more difficult to arrange than when a dog or a cat is involved. There will be some loss of freedom associated with getting a parrot.

Parrots may become aggressive during times of play. You must learn to be aware of your pet's moods and know which signs to take caution of. Things such as pinning of the eyes and fanning of the tail are signs of aggressive behavior.

All parrots, at one time or another, will "test" their owners. They begin to get a little aggressive and try to ignore what it is that you wish them to do. This Monk Parakeet does not want to get off its owner's shoulder.

Hand-feeding is a delicate and time-consuming task. Unless you have a lot of experience, it is best to get a weaned baby parrot.

Parrots need fresh, clean, nutritious foods. These will cost money and require preparation time. All parrots waste food and, in addition, they regularly need to be offered some foods that they may only ingest occasionally. If you are unable to accept this, perhaps a parrot is not for you.

With few individual exceptions, parrots are messy. They fling their foods, play with them, make "soup" in their water bowls, destroy toys and other objects as a necessary exercise. While some parrots may be toilet-trained, and occasionally are neat eaters, a very neat parrot is probably bored, sick, or not offered many of the necessary foods. You should be prepared to clean the cage and the area around it at least daily.

Parrots may need specialized avian veterinary care. You are ethically responsible for providing this care when needed. Some people reason that they won't spend more in vet bills than what they paid for a bird. This is not a responsible attitude and it's similar to refusing to spend any money on a child because conception was free. Even a healthy parrot will have some care and grooming needs.

While parrots can be caged, most require more time and attention than a dog or a cat. Play-time outside the cage is necessary for parrots to stay happy, tame and secure around people. You will probably need to allocate certain spaces for this activity throughout your house. These areas will require cleaning and preparation as well.

All parrots make noise and, occasionally, bite. While some species of parrots are quieter and less aggressive than others, expecting silence (or nothing but sweet talk) and perfect behavior is not realistic. With good socialization, parrots can become wonderful, affectionate companions, and you can learn to forgive

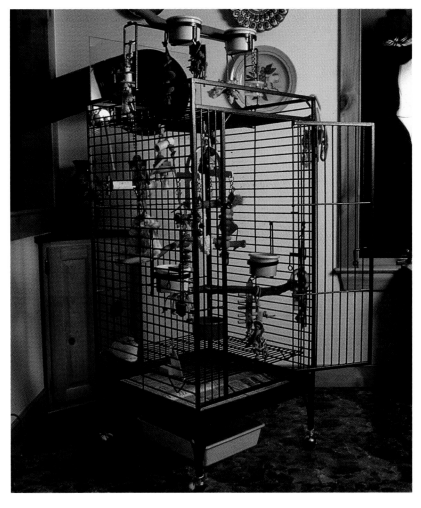

The ideal location for a cage depends on the personality of your bird. A shy, timid parrot may need the protection of the corner of a room. A bold and sociable bird may want to be in the center of activity.

an occasional bite or two. But if you are strict and want a disciplined and obedient pet, you should probably get a puppy instead. This is not to say that parrots should do as they please. Rules are very important for proper socialization. However, they must be set with concern and understanding for the animal's natural tendencies.

You will only get back what you put in. Parrots are individuals with different potentials and social needs. They are highly perceptive and intelligent and can make

Allowing your pet to play with other pets in your house should only be done under your supervision. Even your most trustworthy pet has basic instincts which can be extremely dangerous to your pet parrot.

Hand-fed baby parrots imprint upon humans. Birds raised in this fashion make far better pets than wild-caught or imported birds.

great companions. Like children, they can be raised to be wonderful, or they can be totally spoiled. A responsibly raised, handled parrot is likely to bring much enjoyment to everyone around it. Good planning, realistic expectations, consistency and responsibility will put you on the way to owning and enjoying the best of avian friends.

HAND-FED VERSUS PARENT-RAISED

Birds form social attachments with individuals who look like those who fed them when they were young. This process, called *imprinting*, normally results in birds forming an identity as a member of their group. However, if another species (such as human) provides the feeding during this stage, birds relate to this group as their own. Put very simply, a hand-fed parrot will feel like it belongs with people, more than with other birds. For this reason, they will be more trusting of humans and less stressed around them.

A hand-fed parrot is usually (not always) domestic. This means that it was raised in captivity, rather than caught in the wild. This is important, not only because a wild-caught bird will identify humans as enemies, but because the capture of wild birds for pets should not be supported. Most of the 330 species of parrots in the world are endangered, and the capture of wild birds results in great loss of life due to injury and disease. In addition, these birds are put through a great deal of suffering in transport.

If you ever get tempted to "rescue" a poor, wild-caught bird from an importer, remember that by doing so you are supporting this business. The result for the importer is a sale, and therefore the stock will just be replenished in the same way. In contrast, if you let them know you favor domestic stock, you will be contributing to lowering the demand for imported, wild-caught birds.

Not every supplier will give you the real story behind the bird you are considering. A domestic bird should have a closed band with an identification code that includes information about the breeder, the state and perhaps the year, in addition to an individual number. An imported bird will have an open band (with a seam) that is placed on the bird at the quarantine station. If the bird is not banded, it is important that you trust the supplier. The bird may be stolen or smuggled. Occasionally, owners need to have bands removed to prevent accidents, and there are even some breeders who won't band their birds to avoid this possibility. Some small birds, like budgies and cockatiels, are not often banded.

Even if you know a bird is domestic, you may be told it was hand-fed, when

These parrots' closed bands shows their domestic origin. Bands are slipped over a baby's foot at about two weeks of age. The foot's growth makes it impossible to remove it later without cutting it. Imported birds have an open band, which is applied to each bird after quarantine.

in fact it was parent-raised. A hand-fed bird should not be afraid of people. It may have learned to recognize the person who raised it and refuse to go willingly to a stranger, but it should not panic. Finally, "hand-fed" can't be equated with "properly nurtured and socialized." Some birds are raised with great gentleness and care, they are talked to, petted and not rushed through each feeding. Others, unfortunately, are fed in assembly line fashion, roughly, quickly and without concern. These birds, of course, are not likely to trust people very much. If possible, meet the supplier and observe the feedings. Pay attention to hygiene, gentleness and

setting. Get references. Ask questions from people at the local bird club, or call local vets.

Some very popular species of pet parrots, such as budgies and cockatiels, are frequently sold as

Hand-fed baby parrots learn to depend on humans and are therefore more trusting than a wild-caught or imported bird.

A hand-fed baby parrot should not be afraid of humans. If properly raised, with gentleness and great care, your new pet should be quite social.

parent-raised young because they tame very easily. With these species you don't need to worry about the possibility of getting a wild-caught bird because they have been successfully bred in captivity for decades. As long as you know how to choose healthy and young individuals, which we will discuss later, they are likely to become wonderful pets in a short time.

NEW BABY VERSUS OLDER PET

When you get a baby the individual personality of the bird hasn't fully developed. Also, babies go through some difficult stages, require a lot of time and care, and seem to get themselves in trouble quite often. However, because it is much easier to prevent than to correct behavioral problems such as

A young bird's personality is very influential. It will try many new things and can get into quite a bit of trouble.

screaming, biting and plucking, it's much better raise a parrot well than to reform a "problem" bird.

Not many people part with a well-raised parrot. It is possible, on occasion, to get a wonderful pet from someone who is forced to give it up due to moving, health, or other reasons. These parrots will have trouble dealing with the loss of their families and homes, but if they have had positive experiences with people, they are likely to adapt to a new situation. A lot of patience and an effort to provide the bird with what it's used to will help a great deal. The same cage may provide security, but if this is not possible you should improve on the previous situation. Good accommodations, new toys, varied perches and special treats will soon be appreciated.

SELECTING A SPECIES

Most of the available species of hand-fed parrots can make good pets. However, probably only a few would be right for you. These are some of the questions you may ask yourself to narrow down the choice:

What size? Parrots range in size from tiny to huge. At one end of the spectrum, you have budgies, parrotlets and lovebirds, and at the other the larger macaws and cockatoos. A good way to narrow down your selection is to ask yourself how large a parrot you want or can have. The larger parrots can be dangerous to small children, and even small dogs. They are expensive to purchase and to maintain and require a lot of room and special equipment. A full-size macaw's wing span is well over three feet. Since an adequate cage should

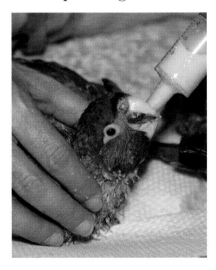

that the frequency with which they move and interact with each other has a different rhythm. Will one bore you? Will the other one drive you crazy? Generally, while activity levels vary among individuals, there are certain characteristics that tend to prevail for each species.

How much talking ability? African Greys are excellent mimics, but usually take one to two years to learn to talk and tend to be quiet when strangers are present. Amazons generally love to show off. Budgies may learn a few words at a very young age. Cockatiels are excellent whistlers. While all parrots have the potential to mimic speech, no matter what you buy, there is no guarantee that your bird will talk.

always allow for comfortable wing-flapping, large macaws are almost impossible to house adequately in most homes. If you get a smaller cage because you plan to have the bird out of it for a good part of the day, remember this must be done every day and requires supervision. I recommend deciding how big a cage you can have, then limiting yourself to a species that would be very comfortable housed in a cage that size.

How active? Some parrots are quiet, some are in constant motion. If you are not familiar with parrots, I suggest you visit a pet store and compare, for example, a budgie or a lovebird with a cockatiel. You will probably notice

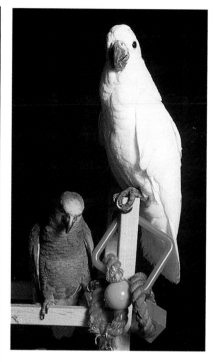

How important are looks? Do you want a rainbow-colored bird, or will you be happy with a pure white cockatoo, or a green parakeet? Some people simply can't resist the beauty of a particular parrot and must take it home.

How important is cuddling? Some birds love to be stroked, others don't tolerate it. Generally, they will relate to you as they would to a member of their flock. Species that engage in a lot of physical contact with each other will be likely to cuddle with their human companions.

How demanding a bird do you want? Some birds are happy to be left in their cages and some will want

to be with you whenever they can. While this will flatter you in the beginning, it may tire you out eventually. Be realistic when estimating the time you will be spending with your bird.

How loud can you tolerate? If you live in an apartment or share living quarters with others, you will need to narrow down your choices to quieter birds. With parrots, *quiet* is a relative term. Make sure you know what it means for each species before you buy. Also, remember that individuals vary a great deal, and keep in mind that a few daily periods of loud vocalizations are necessary for parrots.

How much money can you spend? The equipment you will need may cost just as much, if not more, as

your bird. Add everything up before you decide.

To help you make a decision, here are some brief stereotypes of a few species to help you narrow down your options. Once you have done this, read some more about specific types of birds, or even better, talk with people who own them.

Budgies:

These small parrots are inexpensive and abundant in many colors and varieties. Males are said to learn to talk quite well. They are very active and playful and while they chatter, they are not loud. To choose a young bird look for a dark iris. Males

have a dark blue to purple-pink colored cere (fleshy area above the beak), while females tend to have it light blue to flesh-colored. Budgies are intelligent,

larger pets, or if you want to be able to take your bird outside with supervision, cockatiels may not be the best choice.

Lovebirds:

These beautiful birds are great to watch. They are playful and feisty, and hand-fed birds make great pets. Their call is somewhat loud and high-pitched. They are not known for talking ability. They have a reputation for loosing hand-tameness if not handled at least daily. In pairs they become quite independent and are easy to keep.

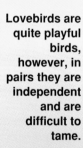

Lovebirds are quite playful birds, however, in pairs they are independent and are difficult to tame.

Parrotlets:

These clowny, tiny birds have a reputation for good talking ability and low noise production. Because they are somewhat demanding and bossy in nature, some people liken them to miniature Amazons. They need plenty of toys and they love baths. Parrotlets like space, but a roomy budgie cage will be adequate. They require more fresh foods than budgies and cockatiels. These birds are easily available as hand-fed pets in several species and their cost is slightly higher than cockatiels.

Quaker or Monk Parakeets:

Playful and affectionate, Quakers may learn to say quite a few words. These are intelligent and very social parrots that may bond strongly to one person and fiercely

The small size of this delightful Barred Parakeet makes it a very pleasant bird to keep.

"protect" that person from all others. They should be handled by everybody in the household daily to avoid this. Their beaks are strong and may inflict painful bites. Quakers are hardy animals and are able to withstand low temperatures with appropriate shelter. Several feral colonies are established in the USA (as far north as Chicago), and cause great damage to crops. They are illegal in several states because of this.

Conures:

Conures form a very large and diverse group of parrots. If you are interested in a conure you should do further reading. Many books are available that cover just conures.

Due to their peaceful and pleasant nature, Monk Parakeets can be tamed quite easily. They do become quite vocal when kept in the house, however, their reputation as screamers is exaggerated.

This Red-masked Conure of the genus *Aratinga* is quite popular. It is from the group which is known to be more vocal, larger, and more colorful.

They come from South America, are sociable and playful. That's as much as they all have in common. They have a reputation for being very loud, but some species are actually pretty quiet. Their size also varies greatly, with some species being smaller than a cockatiel, and some as large as a small macaw. Their coloration and talking ability also varies among species. Broadly, conures can be divided in two groups. The *Aratinga* conures tend to be larger, more colorful, louder, and with better talking ability. *Pyrrhura* conures are smaller and quieter. Prices vary. Because conures have been imported in great numbers for many years, wild-caught birds are still commonly available.

Lories and Lorikeets:

These parrots have recently become more common in aviculture. They are small to medium in size, generally of striking appearance, playful, affectionate and with relatively good talking ability. They used to be avoided because of messy, smelly, liquid droppings that tended to be squirted in and around the cage. Better understanding of their dietary needs has corrected most of this problem. They are known to be mainly pollen eaters, with brushy tongues especially suited for this purpose. Since their special diets were modified, their droppings have become similar to other parrots'. Keep in mind that these special diets need to be provided to sustain health in captivity, and that this implies an additional expense.

Lories and Lorikeets are noted for their extremely playful personalities. Due to their special diet, however, they do require a bit more care than other parrot-like birds.

Senegal Parrot, *Poicephalus senegalus.* Birds of this genus are said to be quite playful and learn to talk quite well. They are of a medium size with a stocky build and, because of their strong beaks, must be housed in cages with a fairly heavy gauge.

Poicephalus Parrots:

This group is formed by nine species of small to medium sized African parrots. Not all of them are common in aviculture. They are all intelligent and able to learn speech, with a somewhat electronic voice. Their talking ability doesn't seem to differ by sex. They are comparatively quiet and quite playful, and hand-fed birds generally make wonderful pets. The most widely available is the Senegal Parrot, a small, stocky bird with a beautiful yellow, green and gray plumage. Meyer's, Red-bellied and Brown-headed parrots are similar in size and personality. The Red-bellied Parrot is sexually dimorphic and known as a better talker. Jardine and Cape parrots are larger, but share some of the characteristics of the smaller *Poicephalus* species. In general, they enjoy a varied diet of fruits, vegetables, nuts, seeds, pellets and table foods. All

The Indian Ringneck is a beautiful bird with good talking ability. It is available in its natural green color, as pictured here, as well as a yellow and a blue mutation.

Psittacula **Parrots:**

These are long-tailed, small to medium sized parrots which originated primarily in Asia. The most common is the Indian Ringneck Parakeet, which is available in its natural green color and in several mutations. Beautiful and moderately priced, they are independent, intelligent and have good talking ability. Their calls can get loud when they mature, but some remain quiet. Some people consider them unsuitable for pets due to their tendency to lose tameness as they develop. Others find this not to be the case with proper and frequent handling.

of these parrots, in spite of their relatively small size, have extremely powerful beaks capable of inflicting serious injury or destroying housewares. They must be socialized properly to become and remain enjoyable pets. Also, because of their strong beaks, many of the cages that would be suitable in terms of their size are not of adequate strength. Larger cages may have bars that are too widely spaced for the size of these parrots. Their cost is moderate for most species, but the need for sturdy equipment represents an additional expense. Some consider many of these parrots unsuitable for households with young children because they have a tendency to react nervously to fast movements.

African Grey Parrots:

Two subspecies, the Congo and the Timneh, are available. Similar in intelligence and talking ability, the Timneh is smaller, darker, with a maroon (as opposed to red) tail, and a horn-colored (rather than black) upper mandible. In addition, the Timneh is less common, somewhat cheaper and, according to many, sweeter than the Congo. These parrots are very intelligent and capable of learning a large vocabulary which they use appropriately. They are playful, affectionate and usually not very loud. They are

African Grey Parrots are known for their intelligence and their ability to mimic speech. Most hand-fed African Greys learn a respectable vocabulary, which they learn to use in the appropriate context.

known to be prone to feather plucking, a potential problem with any parrot. A large cage with varied toys, a good diet, a predictable schedule and a lot of attention may prevent this problem. Also, early socialization that promotes flexibility is crucial. Birds that remain in the same area all day are likely to become very afraid of change. Several play areas throughout the house, trips by car in a pet carrier, short vacations, a familiar boarding cage, exposure to the outdoors, etc., are necessary at a young age to help these intelligent birds become familiar with situations they will encounter sooner or later. Generally, these are demanding pets that require a great deal of interaction to remain happy and enjoyable. They are somewhat expensive.

species that are known for their gentleness and quieter temperaments, while not for their talking potential, are the Lilac-crowned and the Spectacled or White-fronted. Amazons are playful and intelligent and, unlike African Greys, tend to be good performers in front of strangers. All Amazons need plenty of fruits and vegetables in their diets. They may become obese and frail on a diet that is too heavy in seeds and nuts. Prices are in the moderate to expensive range, but they vary greatly by species.

Amazons:

With approximately thirty species, this group is extremely diverse. Generally green and stocky, with a characteristic musty odor, Amazon parrots usually share the ability to produce loud calls. The best talkers are considered to be the Yellow-naped, the Double Yellow-headed and the Blue-fronted Amazons. These birds can be somewhat unpredictable during periods of hormonal fluctuations. They are able to produce serious and disfiguring injuries and generally, are not a good choice for families with young children. Some, however, are extremely loyal and gentle. Two

Pionus Parrots:

Generally smaller than Amazons, but very similar in appearance and smell, these birds share a reddish undertail, and quieter, steadier natures. If you want the playfulness and color of an Amazon without the hormonal swings and the aggression, they are a good choice. *Pionus* Parrots are known for their gentleness and friendliness, as well as their low noise production. Although they are not generally considered good talkers, many do learn good vocabularies. The most commonly available species are the White-capped, the Blue-headed, the Bronze-winged, and the

Maximilian. They are generally less expensive than Amazons. They share with Amazons a need for lots of fruits and vegetables.

Macaws:

Ranging in size from the "minis" (smaller than some conures), to the huge Hyacinth Macaw (over three feet in length), macaws are demanding, playful, intelligent, cuddly and loud. Individuals range from totally tame and sweet to dangerously unapproachable. Hand raised birds usually remain gentle with their families. Children and other pets need to be protected from their powerful beaks. Macaws can easily kill smaller birds in play. Large or small, a macaw is a big commitment, and will generally be quite

expensive to acquire and to keep. Their dietary needs include nuts, vegetables, fruits, breads and seeds.

Cockatoos:

Cockatoos are very intelligent Australian birds. White, pink, salmon, and even black species exist. These birds have limited talking ability but some talk quite well. Their abundant feather dust, which is normal and desirable (as its absence may indicate health problems) may cause or aggravate allergies in people. Cockatoos can be extremely loud and demanding, but they usually love petting and cuddling, making very rewarding pets for the right person. They are powerful chewers that can quickly destroy wood, drywall and

Pionus Parrots are known for gentleness and friendliness, as well as their low noise production.

Macaws are wonderful pets that prove to be quite playful. Because of their large size, they can easily injure smaller birds in play.

furniture. Their undesirable behaviors may be curbed or redirected, but usually not totally eliminated. They are generally expensive to acquire and maintain.

Eclectus Parrots:

These strikingly beautiful, sexually dimorphic parrots can make wonderful pets that are not too loud and learn to talk quite well. They often are just as happy to play by themselves as with their owners. Females, almost unbelievably red colored, have a reputation for not making good pets. However, some who are familiar with both males and females, consider this to be unfounded and actually prefer females. These parrots dislike having their feathers ruffled or scratched, but express affection in other ways. Eclectus Parrots are usually expensive, but their prices have declined recently due to increased availability.

The fact that every parrot is an individual cannot be overemphasized. If you feel very strongly about a quality, such as talking or performing, you may consider adopting an older pet with an established personality. Getting a baby demands acceptance of its individuality. Choosing a

particular species may give you a greater chance that your parrot will resemble your ideal, but it is no guarantee. There are shy Amazons and bold Greys, quiet macaws and loud Senegals; there are some Greys that never learn a word, and female cockatiels with extensive vocabularies. Occasionally, some personality traits can be apparent at an early age. If you have the opportunity to see several babies of the same clutch or species, observe their interaction and their reaction to you. Listen to their vocalizations. You may be able to select some traits from these observations, even before your baby is feathered.

Eclectus parrots are strikingly beautiful birds. The female is bright red in color while the male exhibits vivid kelly green plumage.

Salmon-crested Cockatoo, *Cacatua moluccensis*. Cockatoos love to be handled and require a great deal of affection from their owners. Those who are away from their home for the better part of the day should not consider one of these birds.

A good pet store will be well-stocked with specialty foods, accessories and toys, in addition to a selection of young birds.

SELECTING A SUPPLIER

Most parrots are purchased from a pet store or a private breeder. Do not consider any pet stores or breeders that don't demonstrate compassion and concern for their birds through their actions. Cages, and food and water bowls should always be clean. Appropriate foods and toys should be present. Birds should have ample space and should be protected from harassment by strangers. Too many birds packed close together may increase disease transmission and stress.

Pet stores usually charge higher prices, but the difference is insignificant over the life of a pet. It is most important to pay attention to the quality of the care birds receive to produce healthy, well adjusted pets. If you get a sickly companion, you may lose a lot of money on vet bills, or even a replacement pet. Meanwhile, your family will have to weather some stressful times.

A bird purchased at a pet store is usually much more exposed to people, but this may work for or against the making of a good pet. A sensitive store manager will protect the bird and oversee all contact with strangers. On the other hand, a poorly managed store may leave baby birds vulnerable to abuse, teasing and rough handling. At a breeder's facility, babies usually remain in a "nursery" until they are purchased.

Exposure to other birds also needs to be considered. A good store will have a limited number of birds, separately housed by clutch. However, birds of all kinds and origins may be present, increasing the chances of disease transmission. Many breeders choose to specialize in certain types of birds, for example Australian parakeets or

If you have the opportunity to see several birds of the same species be sure to observe their interaction with each other as well as with you.

African parrots, because birds from the same area tend to share immunity to certain ailments. Contacting the local avicultural association for references about a supplier is always a good idea. If you don't know where to begin, call a veterinarian's office and ask for advice.

Hygiene is extremely important. Inspect cages and brooders very carefully. Are they clean? What types of bedding or cage linings are used? Some linings, such as newspaper, may look dirty soon after having been changed, but you should be able to differentiate fresh droppings and food debris from old ones. An advantage of paper is that you can observe the appearance of the droppings. Other types of lining, such as processed corn or litter, hide droppings and debris very well and may appear clean even days after a cleaning, but harbor harmful bacteria and molds.

Do the birds have toys? Do very young babies have soft surfaces, such as tissue, paper towels or cloth? How are the feedings handled? Is the area reasonably

Pet stores and breeders will often house different species of birds together.

uncluttered or is it packed with cages and birds? What weaning foods are used? Do you see fresh greens, fruits, vegetables? What dry foods are available? Are the water bowls clean? Parrots often dip food in their water, creating quite a mess, but it takes a while for the water to become cloudy and murky. You should be able to differentiate just-messed-up water from old, dirty water.

Is the supplier willing to answer all your questions without pressure, or does he or she seem too eager to get rid of the bird? A good breeder or store manager should care more about the bird's future than about making a sale. If good care went into the baby, the caretaker should have developed some attachment to it and show concern for the bird.

The work of a good breeder or store manager is admirable. It is a lot harder to do this job properly than poorly. Fortunately, there are plenty of suppliers that will actually discourage you from getting a bird if they don't think it is appropriate for you. Tell the supplier what your needs are. If you don't feel comfortable and trusting, find another supplier.

Take note of the environment the baby you wish to purchase is housed in. Fresh foods and seeds should be a part of the diet. This Umbrella Cockatoo has a feast in front of it waiting to be eaten.

Hand feeding baby parrots is a labor-intensive and risky task better left to the most experienced. A four-week old Eclectus, such as this one, may require six feedings a day.

SELECTING A HEALTHY BABY

While there is no sure way to select a healthy baby just by looking at it, there are certain characteristics that are best avoided. A sick baby spends less time preening. Often, this results in poor feather condition. Healthy birds never have feces stuck around the vent area. All babies occasionally drag their tail over droppings, causing some smearing of feathers, but this is very different from feces sticking to feathers surrounding the vent.

Droppings may vary a lot, particularly in unweaned babies. They may be more watery than in adult birds due to excess water in the formula and weaning foods. However, they should still resemble parrot droppings. You should be able to distinguish three parts in the droppings: a formed portion (stools), a clear liquid portion (urine) and a whitish portion (urates).

Most baby parrots lose weight just before they wean. Be sure that the baby you purchase has good weight on it and bring it back to the supplier after a week to be sure that it has not lost any weight. The two youngsters pictured here do not seem to be under-weight.

Healthy baby parrots sleep a lot, but also show various periods of active play.

Repeated droppings without clear liquid indicate dehydration. Mucous or blood droppings are clearly abnormal. Certain colored pellets may cause reddish or orange droppings and urine.

Babies tend to sleep a lot, but they should show frequent periods of bouncy play as they approach weaning. If there are several babies in a group, these periods tend to be synchronized. If a baby sleeps in a corner while everyone is having fun, a problem may be present. A good appetite is a healthy sign. It's always a good idea to observe a feeding.

Stress marks are lines of abnormal growth that resemble clear or gray streaks across a feather. Some species of parrots are more prone to them than others, but in general they develop in response to a stress, such as a bacterial infection. While a couple of marked feathers may be insignificant, it is best to avoid heavily marked babies. Abnormally shaped or bent feathers are also a worrisome sign. It is important to differentiate these feather abnormalities from broken feathers. Broken feathers (quite common in babies) will be replaced with new ones within a year, at the first molt. Abnormal feathers, however, are sometimes the first sign of Psittacine Beak and Feather Disease (PBFD) and indicate possible problems with the entire clutch.

Most babies lose weight during weaning, but their chest muscles should remain level with the sternum. If the breastbone feels sharp, the baby is too

This Mexican Red-headed Amazon is a fine example of what a healthy bird looks like. It has good feather condition, a well-aligned beak, clear eyes, no discharge from the nostrils, and good weight to its body.

thin. This could be temporary, but it is best to observe it for a while.

The beak should be well aligned. A bird with beak abnormalities is certain to require special care throughout its life. Suppliers sometimes sell these birds at a very reduced price to avoid destroying them. If you get a bird with a maligned beak take it to an avian vet immediately. Some beak abnormalities can be corrected.

Legs should be parallel on standing. A bird with one leg at an angle has an abnormality that may not interfere with mobility and pet potential. A few toes may have deformities or may be missing totally or partially. This is usually of no consequence to the bird. However, should you desire to breed your bird in the future, you should know that missing or abnormal toes may prevent successful mating. On the other hand, a discount due to a minor foot abnormality may allow you to afford the pet of your dreams.

Eyes and nostrils should be completely clear and free of discharge. The mouth and tongue should lack whitish spots, which may indicate yeast infections.

Finally, pay attention to behavior and personality. The bounciest baby of the clutch is likely to be more active in the future. The bird's response to you and your handling may also influence your decision. While impulse decisions are to be avoided, a baby that your heart can't say no to is usually off to a good start.

It is also a good idea to select a veterinarian prior to getting your bird. Local bird clubs, pet stores or breeders should be able to give you names of vets who treat birds in your area. These "avian" vets have special equipment and medications in addition to

Most baby parrots sleep for long periods of time during the day, however, they should show frequent periods of bouncy play.

special training and experience. Certification of avian vets is in its early stages; a more important factor is the vet's experience and interest in birds. Select someone whose practice consists of at least 25% birds. In addition to wildlife care and rehabilitation, make sure parrots form a significant part of the avian patients. Many knowledgeable vets lack the practical skill of handling a parrot, making proper examination and procedures impossible. In addition, a vet who is skillful in handling will cause less stress to your bird.

PREPARING FOR THE ARRIVAL

THE CAGE

A good cage is the most important piece of equipment you will buy. You will not regret buying the largest and best cage you can accommodate and afford. It will last many years. It should be safe and comfortable for your bird to live in it, easy for you to clean and pleasant to look at. A cage is necessary for healthy socialization. Some people erroneously think that a bird may be happier "free." The cage defines the bird's territory and it is indispensable to maintain a safe environment for your bird during unsupervised times.

Square or rectangular cages are better choices than round or odd-shaped ones. Round cages have been associated with neurotic behaviors, such as continuous turning and pacing. One possible reason for this may be size, rather than shape. People usually think of a 2' diameter round cage as equivalent to a 2' by 2' square one. However, while both cages require that you give up the same amount of usable living space, the round one provides your

Baby parrots such as this Goffin's Cockatoo often enjoy being handled. Cuddling a bird in such a manner often makes visits to the veterinarian and other outings more tolerable.

A large swing door and feeding trays that are accessible from the outside are nice features to have in a bird cage. They not only make caring for your pet easier on you, but on the bird as well.

A round cage should be of an ample diameter in order to give the bird you wish to keep plenty of room to exercise. A cage this size is suitable to house one budgie or a lovebird.

pet with little more than three quarters of the area of the square one. In addition, square and rectangular cages are easier to line with newspaper and to fit with accessories.

While there are many good cage manufacturers, it's hard to find the ideal cage. Manufacturers sometimes market cages with names such as "Amazon Palace" or "Macaw's Haven." Pay no attention to these names. These cages may be of adequate size for much smaller birds.

First, find out the proper bar strength and bar spacing for the bird you will be getting. This may limit your choices but it's very important. A flight cage for finches may be big enough for a parakeet, but it may not survive its beak.

On the other hand, an Amazon cage may be of nice size for a Senegal, but the bars may be placed too far apart. This may allow for its head to get stuck, possibly causing injury or death.

Once you determine bar spacing and strength, look for the largest possible cage you can accommodate and afford, with the following features, in order of importance:

Sliding tray:

Some cages must be lifted off the tray for cleaning. Day after day, you will regret this. I can't emphasize enough how important it is to get a cage that is easy to clean. Your parrot should live many years. You may have no problem bending,

A play pen top is a nice feature to have on a cage because it allows your pet parrot to play outside the cage yet does not require you to purchase a separate unit.

lifting and twisting now, but you will eventually get the flu or a back ache, or need to rely on others every once in a while. You will appreciate simple procedures then.

Large swing door:
This also aids in cleaning. It is difficult to reach the inside of a cage through small doors. It is also difficult to get your parrot in and out. The door latch should be parrot-proof.

Floor grate:
All parrots should have a grate to avoid contact with feces and ingestion of contaminated foods. Lack of a grate gives parrots a chance to eat cage bedding or lining, such as

All birds naturally gnaw on wood in the wild. This pleasure should not be denied to a parrot kept in a home as a pet. Be sure to supply your pet with plenty of natural branches to gnaw upon.

There are many different sizes and styles of bird carriers available at your local pet store. These make transporting your pet easy and safe.

for cleaning. This is particularly convenient with large cages.

Horizontal and vertical bars:
Parrots like to climb up horizontal bars and slide down vertical ones. Both types of bars are desirable, but not necessary. If you find the cage you want, but it has only vertical bars, you may hang a couple of ladders on the sides. If, on the other hand, it has only horizontal bars, you may hang a couple of sliding and climbing vertical toys from the roof of the cage.

newspaper with inks. Some argue that parrots need to walk on a flat surface, or that their legs may get caught in the grate. Young, clumsy babies may need the grate removed or covered until they become comfortable walking on the bars. I give my parrots a small, flat surface on the floor of their cages, such as a siding brick. This provides them with a landing platform to play or eat at the bottom of the cage, and with a place to scratch their nails and beak. It should be placed where droppings are not likely to fall, such as far from areas below perches.

Casters:
Casters allow for easy moving of cages, necessary

Swing-out or slide-out feeders:
These feeders are not completely necessary, but are a good feature when you have to leave your parrot under someone else's care. Many people are afraid of beaks, and many parrots bite when a

stranger intrudes into the cage. These feeders may save stress to your sitter and your pet.

Playpen top:

Birds love to come out and play on top of their cages. The more amenities provided with the cage, the less you will have to buy. If the cage has a flat top, but no playpen, screw-on playpens are available. However, be aware that your parrot will need other play areas away from the cage to prevent excessive territoriality.

Lock-down or appropriately heavy bowls:

At least three bowls will be needed in the cage, for water, pellets and seeds, and fresh foods. Parrots can lift and drop very heavy

Heavy crock dishes are difficult for birds to lift and spill over. These, or other lock down types, are advisable for larger birds.

bowls. In addition to the mess, this can cause shattering and injury, or may leave your pet without water during your absence. Make sure the bowls are non-porous and easy to clean, preferably dishwasher safe.

You may wish to purchase some toys at the same time that you purchase your baby, however, it would be wise not to introduce these into your parrot's cage until it settles in and is eating well.

Most parrots need to work for their food in the wild. If yours is not interested in vegetables and fruits served in a bowl, try serving them on a skewer attached to a toy or a swing.

If you wish to have your pet parrot step onto your hand do not be intimidated when it shies away. Gently, but firmly, take the bird by both feet from off of its perch and hold it on your hand while talking softly.

Natural perches:

Most cages come with inadequate perches that should be replaced. A few manufacturers supply appropriately sized, natural wood perches. In most cases, you will need to get nicely shaped branches with variable widths. This is important to maintain healthy feet throughout the years. If you are bringing home a young baby, place the perches very low in the cage to avoid hard falls. Provide your bird with different perching levels and interesting paths. Half-perches provide more spring than full perches. It's a good idea to provide both. Also, an additional pedicure perch will pay off by saving you a lot of nail grooming.

Swings:

These are important for coordination, balance and fun. Many styles are available, including some fitted with pedicure perches. Usually, they must be purchased separately.

ADDITIONAL SUPPLIES

Bird carrier:

Standard pet carriers are available in many sizes. Any one of these may be converted into an appropriate bird carrier by simply fitting it with a half perch. Plastic carriers may be appropriate for small parrots, but very large birds may need an all metal travel cage. You may use a small layer of hay or pine shavings on the floor of the

Bird carriers are available from your local pet shop in various sizes. Be sure to purchase one that will fit the size bird you have comfortably.

carrier to absorb droppings. Because water may spill and chill your bird, it should not be provided in the carrier. Slices of apples, fresh peppers, grapes, celery or cucumbers, provide moisture without that danger. Also, never hang toys in the carrier, since they may injure your bird during a trip.

Toys:

Toys are very important to prevent boredom and negative behaviors. Parrots that have nothing to do may overpreen, pluck their feathers or develop other undesirable habits. You can buy toys or make them, but safety has to be your first priority. Toys made for a small bird may be unsafe for a large parrot. Always check toys for possible safety problems: some chains can catch toes and beaks; some bells may

Parrots require time alone in their cage, however, they should have toys within to stimulate them.

There are many household items that are safe for your bird to play with and which will give it hours of enjoyment. This Nanday Conure is having a blast playing with an old toothbrush.

In the wild, parrots feed their young for very long periods after fledgling and gradually teach them to get their own food. Human caretakers must play this role with hand-fed parrots.

cause beaks to get stuck; some fabrics may become frayed, causing fibers to wrap around toes; some paints and varnishes may be toxic; some materials may be eaten causing impaction; long leather straps or ropes may strangle birds...The list is endless. Be reasonable. With parrots, like with children, you should minimize risks but you can't eliminate them totally. If unsure about a toy, use it outside the cage, where your bird will always play with supervision.

Playpen:

You will need a portable play area with at least a perch, a cup and a toy. This will be handy for traveling and useful around your home.

Foods:

Ask your bird supplier to tell you exactly what the bird is eating. While birds adapt to diet changes and need variety, it's best to stick to the same diet for a while. This will give your new pet some continuity, and it will give you one less thing to worry about.

Boarding cage:

It is a good idea to get a small parrot cage as soon as possible. If you are choosing a small bird, this cage can also be used as a carrier. This will be necessary for vacations, boarding and short trips. In addition, they are a good emergency item. You never know when a bad weather warning, a fire, a chemical spill, a power failure or other unexpected problem may force you to move your bird without planning or preparation. If you fit this cage with a good perch, a

Parrots are very inquisitive creatures which will investigate their surroundings once they are comfortable in them.

swing, a toy, a small cage-top perch and a heavy crock, your bird will be safe whenever you need to use it. It is a good idea to accustom your pet to this cage from a young age by, for example, providing playtime on or around it for a while, and later using it for a trip or two.

Night light:
If your bird gets startled in the dark, it may get injured before it becomes reoriented and calm. A dim light assists a bird in finding its way back to the perch and recognizing its surroundings. The best night lights are automatic and will go on as soon as it gets dark and off as soon as there is enough light. With one of these you won't need to worry about remembering to turn it on and off, or to get home before dark.

While you will be getting other items periodically, this is all you need to prepare for the arrival of your new pet.

Baby parrots that have just weaned will often regress and begin to beg for food. It is important to offer your new pet many different types of soft foods that are easy for it to digest during this time.

THE TRIP HOME

Your bird's supplier is the best source of recommendations for a safe and comfortable trip home. A bird that is not perching securely may be more comfortable in a carrier fitted with a towel, rather than with a perch. If you are inexperienced, ask your supplier for a brief practical lesson on handling, including picking up, holding and petting. Before you take off with the baby make sure you observe its droppings for later comparison. Observation of its environment is also important. Is the food placed low in the cage? How about the perches? What are the favorite treats? What toys are familiar? Don't forget the phone number of your bird's supplier, and make sure to call with any questions. Also, obtain some food from the supplier and make sure wings have been clipped.

It is always easier to go with someone else to pick up your pet. This is very helpful to keep an eye on the baby during the trip. Also, in extreme weather it

This baby African Grey is ready to spend some time in a specially adapted cage. The seemingly bare bulge on this bird's chest is a very full crop.

To prevent your bird from becoming a "one person bird," have everyone in the family handle the bird as well as share in the care.

allows for at-the-door pick up, saving the baby from exposure. If you need to stop for gas or supplies, do it before you pick up the baby. Make this journey as brief and gentle as it can be for your new friend, who will undoubtedly be scared and stressed. Driving smoothly and talking softly during the trip will be reassuring to a hand-raised bird.

When you get home, hold your bird close to your body for a while, as long as this seems comfortable to the baby. You may have read many times that the best thing to do is to leave the pet alone in its cage. This generally applies to wild-caught birds, who are very afraid of people. For a new baby that has just been separated from its clutch mates and "mother,"

need some time to get used to you to tolerate being held. Now and always, the most important element of a good relationship with your bird is *good listening*: to pay attention to what your bird is communicating through body language or expression and to be sensitive to it.

While your new pet is not likely to eat immediately, offering foods that are familiar will identify you as a caretaker and friend. For the first few days offer these foods inside and outside the cage. Many birds are scared of a new cage and won't eat there. However, they may be comfortable enough to eat on a counter with you. Toys hanging close to food bowls, or crocks that are

body contact is likely to be stress reducing. Of course, observe the pet's reactions and don't force any unwanted contact right away. Your bird may see you as a stranger and may

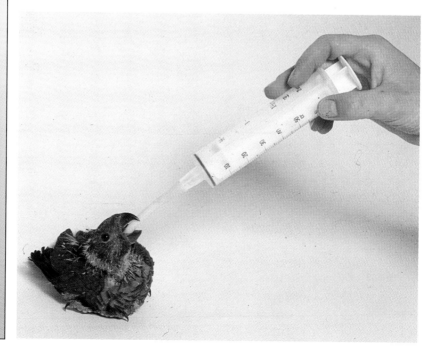

wash your hands well before doing this, because bacteria and yeast can be transmitted to the baby in this way. Soft, warm foods are appealing to babies, even if they have been weaned to a hard diet such as pellets, seeds, fruits and vegetables. In addition, if a baby is feeling insecure, it won't spend much time eating. Soft foods can be ingested faster and more efficiently, preventing weight loss. Sleeping a lot, being relatively quiet and not eating much, are all normal for a just-moved baby. If your bird does not eat at all for a full day, however, you need to consult the supplier immediately.

very different from what the bird has been used to, may also keep your pet from eating. Make sure that bowls are not too deep and that they are placed where the baby can reach them. For many babies, this is the floor of the cage.

Many babies regress a little during times of stress. That is, a baby that has weaned may go back to begging for a feeding for a couple of days. Talk with your supplier about the feeding routines. Many people who hand raise parrots move from a spoon or a syringe to finger feeding towards weaning. Sometimes offering a little soft food between your fingers is all you need to do to get the baby eating on its own. Make sure you

Some parrots get carried away, and become so excited when they play that they could take a nasty fall. Be sure to provide long hanging toys in your pet's cage to prohibit such accidents.

Toys that hang down and are long are good to have in the cage in case your pet loses its balance.

Baby parrots need time to rest, preen, play and eat. This Hispanolian Amazon is resting comfortably in the confines of his cage.

It is a good idea to consult an avian vet during the first week that your baby is home. Any problems found should be discussed with your supplier. Remember that even the best breeders or stores may unknowingly have birds with ailments such as a bacterial infection. Some of these infections are very common and they don't indicate that you got a sickly bird or that your supplier did something wrong. However, a caring supplier will appreciate the information and use it to the benefit of the remaining birds. You also may ask your supplier if you can obtain cultures of your bird's droppings just before bringing it home.

This is a time to spoil your baby a little by providing many different foods and treats. The bird will identify you as a protector and caretaker and will feel comfortable soon. To prevent raising a "one person bird" get everyone in the family to share in the care. This will help your baby become less anxious about other people too. However, resist the temptation of holding the baby all day long, then drastically reducing contact once the novelty wears out. Begin setting the routine that will be followed.

Too much attention can be detrimental at this stage. Babies need time to rest, preen, play with their toys and entertain themselves alone. They also need to develop a sense of self control by learning routines. It is a good idea, for example, to keep wake up time and sleep time constant. Remember that most parrots come from tropical areas where night and day are close to twelve hours each. Try to provide twelve hours of quiet rest at night, preferably away from bright lights and loud noise.

Keep a balance between respect for your pet's

routine and a need for flexibility. Your pet will live for a long time and it is not realistic to attempt, for example, to have supper at home every day at the same exact time. A bird that learns to expect how each day will evolve, may become extremely stressed with any change. Ideally, your pet will feel secure that someone will always clean the cage and provide clean water and food, that there will always be some playtime with company outside the cage, that when its owners leave the house they will always come back, and that it won't ever be hurt by anybody in the family. Everything else may change, and your bird should be able to adapt to it. Guests' visits, parties, weather storms and home improvements are just a few examples of stresses your bird will have to cope with.

PREVENTING AND DETECTING PROBLEMS

QUARANTINE

If you already own another bird or birds, you may have considered a quarantine period. The prevailing recommendation calls for at least forty-five days spent in a different room, preferably distant from your other birds. The problem with quarantine is that it adds stress to the bird by limiting contact with its family, it requires a second change of location and it provides very few safeguards. Many of the most feared diseases have a much longer latency period than forty-five days. Psittacine Beak and Feather Disease, for example, can appear more than three years after exposure. Other diseases, such as Proventricular Dilation Syndrome, may have even longer latency periods.

If you own only one or two older birds that have been isolated from other birds for at least a few months, an informal, one-sided quarantine already

If you intend to house several birds together, or even in the same room, it is wise to quarantine them initially to be sure that no illnesses can infect the rest of your stock.

A baby parrot's immune system is not fully resistant to germs. It is a good idea to inspect the conditions under which your baby came from before you bring it home.

has been provided. The situation from which the new bird comes is also important to make a sound decision about quarantine. If you purchase your bird at a pet store, a quarantine period should be observed at least until a vet examines your pet and culture results are back. On the other hand, if you have purchased from a breeder who has a surgically clean nursery, with just a couple of separately housed clutches of babies, it may be safe to assume that your pet has been quarantined during the hand-feeding stage.

Breeders, however, should always observe respectful quarantine periods. Since they are likely to have many birds in close quarters undergoing stressful periods, such as breeding or raising young, no degree of caution is excessive. Babies are vulnerable to disease and must be protected as much as possible. It is always best to take your bird to an avian vet for an initial exam immediately after acquiring it. If the vet detects any problem, you will have a chance to negotiate with the supplier before you are strongly attached to the bird. If everything is fine, you will get peace of mind

and an opportunity to establish a relationship with a vet, should a medical emergency arise later.

ACCIDENT PREVENTION

Some parrots, such as African Greys, are extremely clumsy through their first year. Some other parrots become quite self-sufficient in a very short time. It is a good idea to take precautions until you know the capabilities of your new pet. Provide only a small amount of water in the water dish until you are absolutely certain that your bird could get out of the dish, should it fall in. Place at least one perch very close to the bottom of the cage, and food dishes on the floor or close to it. As soon as you are confident that your bird can master

heights, you can rearrange the cage. As you provide higher perches and swings, prepare for possible falls. Hang long toys from swings and high perches to provide your bird with something to hold on to when losing balance. These toys can act as mock vines, giving a "jungle" character to the cage.

If your bird is very young, provide a folded towel in a corner of the cage for resting. The towel should not have open weave loops where toenails or toes may get caught. Cotton diapers or kitchen towels work well. Change it often and assist your new friend with grooming by cleaning soiled feathers with moist tissue or cotton balls. While it would be very worrisome for a fully grown bird to need help

Perches of variable width, such as these of natural wood, are necessary for foot health.

with this, it is not unusual for young babies to be quite inept at preening and prone to walking on their droppings or food dishes. You should see steady improvement in this respect quite early.

Parrots that are just starting to perch may still sleep on the cage floor for a few days or even weeks. This is normal in a baby but not in an older bird. A return to this behavior after it has been abandoned for a while may be cause for concern. If this happens, examine your bird carefully for any signs of restricted movement, injuries or pain. If the bird seems fine, is easily arousable and interested in play, eats well and produces normal droppings, it may simply be a temporary regression to safer patterns of behavior.

It is never too early to establish rules that will result in safer habits later on. One of these rules is making clear that the floor of your home is not part of your bird's territory. A bird on the floor could be easily stepped on and killed. In addition, it may wander to areas and objects that have not been "bird-proofed," such as electrical wiring, household chemicals, toxic paints and fibers, or another animal's food or territory. If your bird comes down to the floor, consistently return it to its

at the tip of the coverts, starting with the second outer primary and ending with the last secondary;

• clipping 5 to 8 primaries starting with the third outer primary, at the tip of the coverts.

The first method alters the appearance of the wings, eliminating the crossed wing tips over the tail. The second one is more difficult to perform, check and maintain, and the bird may regain flight by replacing just a couple of feathers. The third one results in many injuries when birds catch the outer primaries between cage bars, or injure wing tips while flapping, since the shock absorption normally provided by the rest of the primaries is absent. In spite of appearances, this author uses the first method on both wings, because she is most comfortable with it.

The degree of clipping must be tailored to each bird. In general, elongated birds with long tails need more primaries cut to lose flight, while plumper, shorter birds, need fewer. Your supplier or avian vet should be able to recommend a method for your bird. Since clipping is reversible after each molt, your observations and your experience with a method will help you decide whether to stick to it or to modify it in the future.

Never attempt to clip

It is important that you bring your pet bird to an experienced handler or an avian veterinarian to have its wings or nails clipped.

This Blue and Gold Macaw can enjoy the outdoors with proper wing clipping and supervision. Pet birds make easy prey for cats, dogs, raptors and other animals. Never leave your pet alone outside.

wings without having seen it done first, and being absolutely certain that you know exactly what to do. Learn to recognize *blood feathers*, which should never be cut. These are feathers that are still growing and have an active blood supply. They are noticeable only by checking the underside of the wing, and they resemble small bluish plastic tubes. Always have the assistance of another person to restrain the bird. Any sudden movement may cause you to injure your pet. Also, be ready to stop bleeding, should an accident occur. Your local pet store can sell you styptic powder, which is a coagulant. If you don't have styptic powder, cornstarch may work in an emergency. Seek immediate vet care if bleeding continues. Any blood loss is serious for a bird.

Always "test" a clipping by gently tossing the bird on a bed or a couch from a distance of a foot or two. The bird should be able to flutter down without gaining height. Any more

The beak of most parrots generally does not require clipping. As long as plenty of gnawing material is available, there is no cause to worry. Take note of what a proper beak looks like and consult an expert or avian vet at the first sign of change.

Nail trimming is rarely necessary when proper perches are provided.

lift may call for clipping of additional feathers. A more drastic drop may indicate overclipping. While this may be reversed at the next molt, you need to be aware of it to prevent falls that may injure your bird, and to correct it in the future.

TOENAIL CARE

Overgrown toenails can cause accidents by getting caught in fabrics or toys. Pedicure perches and swings help prevent this problem. They are a good investment. They will save time, stress and money for grooming needs. These perches, available in many sizes, are half-perches that

bolt to the side of the cage. It is recommended to install them high in the cage, since birds tend to favor height. Your bird should always have other kinds of perches too, such as wood of variable widths. It would be cruel to force a bird to stand on a single, hard, cold perch. However, if you provide variety, you don't need to worry about comfort. Whenever your bird is on the cement perch, it's out of choice. In the wild, birds often land on rocks and hard terrain; that's why they do so well without toe care parlors.

If you ever need to clip your bird's toenails, I recommend that you take your bird to a vet or specialized store, at least

the first time. It is a good idea to bring your own towel to restrain the bird. Towels that have been used with other birds may transmit disease.

BEAK CARE

If your bird has a normally aligned beak and if you are providing appropriate chewing materials and a cement perch, you should never have to worry about beak trimming. Occasionally, minor adjustments may be necessary, but in that case you should take the bird to an avian vet. If you cause a beak injury, it can be serious or even fatal to your pet. Fractures and profuse bleeding could occur. In addition, you may cause a lot of pain to your bird.

Beak overgrowth also may be an early sign of disease. Because any beak problem is potentially life threatening in terms of future feeding ability, always take your pet to a vet if you suspect anything abnormal with its beak.

OUTDOOR PLAY

The outdoors can be enjoyable but very risky to pet birds. Safety comes first, but that doesn't mean you should totally rule out outside play. Proper clipping can prevent escape for most birds, but some, such as cockatiels, are so aerodynamic that they would have to be severely trimmed to prevent flight. In addition, because of their very small size, they are particularly vulnerable to injury. For birds like these, outside time is safe only inside a cage or aviary. For stockier parrots, uncaged outside play is possible with great caution.

Beak and toenail clipping should only be performed by an experienced handler or an avian veterinarian.

It is important that you check your pet's flying ability every time you take it out. Birds are strong flyers and can gain lift when only one or two feathers have grown in.

Predation by cats, dogs and wild animals is one of the main causes of pet bird deaths. Always maintain proper wing-clipping and remain at an arm's length if you take the bird outside.

First, you should check your parrot's wings *every single time you take it out.* New primaries should be clipped *one by one* as they replace themselves,

rather than when the wings are fully replaced. Escapes are very common due to lack of discipline in clipping maintenance.

Second, birds will fly by reflex when startled, so it is crucial that your clipped bird always remains surrounded by a safe area of great radius. A fall into a brook, a camp fire, a busy road, a thorny thicket, a marsh, or simply from a high area such as a raised deck or balcony, can all be fatal to a clipped bird. *Always check for safe surroundings.*

Third, your bird is easy prey to cats, raccoons, hawks, owls, foxes and other animals. It could take

When your pet is perched outdoors be sure it is under safe conditions. It should be wing-clipped, and in no danger of being attacked by cats or dogs.

It is best to supply only a small amount of water in your pet's bath to be certain that it cannot fall and drown.

just a few unsupervised seconds for your pet to be taken by a predator. **Never, ever leave your pet alone outside,** not even to go get a glass of water or to pick up the phone. In an emergency, take the bird with you. Even inside a screened porch an uncaged pet bird should be supervised often. Many animals (even your pet) can easily break through screens.

Provided that you can take all these precautions, there is no reason why you can't enjoy a picnic with your pet bird, take a walk around the yard, or have dinner on an outside deck. When the weather is pleasant, birds usually enjoy the fresh air and new surroundings. Just remember that your pet

needs you at an arm's length to remain safe.

Since most parrot cages should be too big to carry comfortably, it is a good idea to get a smaller cage for outside play. The outdoors can be enjoyed more safely from a cage,

It is a good idea to have a smaller cage to transfer your pet parrot into for short trips or picnics outside. Such a cage should be well equipped with interesting toys of different types.

and if your bird ever needs to be boarded, taken on a trip or moved in an emergency, you will have a portable home that feels safe and familiar. You may equip this cage with special toys, treats and swings to make up for the cramped quarters. Also, if you notice your bird appears nervous outside, you may cover the top of the cage with edible branches or a towel for added security. For a bird that has always had a ceiling over its cage, the open sky means danger. Even if you decide to have your bird uncaged outside, a cage comes in handy when you can't provide constant supervision or when young guests are present.

NUTRITION

Much of the current knowledge on bird nutrition comes from poultry research. Additional research has been done on some species, such as cockatiels, but little scientific information exists about the needs of other parrots. Because there are about 330 species of parrots that range broadly in habits, size, range and habitat, we shouldn't readily infer that what applies to one will apply to all. Many pelleted diets and seed mixes claim to be "nutritionally balanced" or "complete," however, a diet which consists of only seed or only pellets is dangerous to all birds.

Good nutrition is important. Birds can live for years on a bad diet, but in the long run their lives are shortened and their health suffers. Variety is always of benefit, not only nutritionally but mentally.

overemphasized this by presenting seed as a dangerous food. If you read the ingredients listed on pelleted foods, you will discover that they are mostly seed of one type or another. What is dangerous to a bird is not seed or pellets, but *only* seed or pellets. It is the *exclusion of other foods* that is likely to cause long-term problems. Pet owners that feed pure diets of these types may face problems in the future.

I don't believe in forcing any diet on a bird, because the bird's choice of foods among a wide variety of items is more likely to be right for that bird than a "balanced" commercial diet. I do believe in giving every bird

A pure seed diet is high in fat and deficient in vitamin A, calcium and many other nutrients. Pellet manufacturers have

Allowing your pet parrot to eat the foods that you enjoy reinforces the bond between you.

Baby parrots that are not yet weaned should have a dish of foods in front of them at all times so that they may begin to learn how to eat on their own. Soft foods are easier for young birds to handle and digest.

A well-balanced diet is essential to your pet's good health. There are many seed and pellet mixtures available from your local pet shop that will supply your parrot with the necessary dietary requirements. Photo courtesy of Kaytee.

as many foods as possible, selecting all the items from fresh, natural sources. However, there are a few foods that should be fed moderately: chocolate, caffeinated drinks, alcohol and avocado. The greasy, sugary or salty foods that we would label as "junk food" should only be fed occasionally. In addition, we should be careful to wash all vegetables and fruits to remove pesticides, avoid feeding plants or branches that might have been sprayed with chemicals, and thoroughly cook animal products such as eggs, meats and bones.

While almost all greens are good, lettuce (particularly iceberg lettuce) has virtually no nutritional value. Chicory, spinach, collard greens, carrot and beet tops, kale, broccoli, watercress, dandelions, plantain, parsley and basil are all good. Green and red peppers, cherry tomatoes, peas in the shell, green beans, carrots, sweet potatoes and okra are usually well liked.

Treats which are fun to eat as well as nutrtious are available from your local pet store. Photo courtesy of Kaytee.

If you have access to trees that are never sprayed, you can also offer twigs and branches. Apple and other fruit trees (maple, birch, beech, spruce, Canadian

hemlock, mountain olive, raspberry, blueberry and ash) are safe. Avoid rhododendron and azalea family plants, yews and any trees and bushes you are not sure about.

Offer *at least* two kinds of leaf greens and two other different vegetables or fruits a day, and vary them at least weekly. Growing a garden is a great way to assure a fresh and inexpensive organic supply.

In general, if you eat a good diet, you won't need to buy many special foods for your bird. Feeding some of your meals in a little bowl will provide a good supplement to your pet's diet and present an opportunity for social bonding. Eating together reinforces the feeling of belonging to a "flock."

Macaws have no problem opening the hard shells of nuts; for smaller parrot-like birds it may be best to crack it part of the way.

Some parrots refuse to eat fresh fruits and vegetables but will eat them cooked or dried. Remember that wet foods should be discarded from your pet's cage after a few hours.

There are many natural and safe toys available from your local pet shop that will satisfy your parrot's chewing and climbing habits. Photo courtesy of Penn Plax.

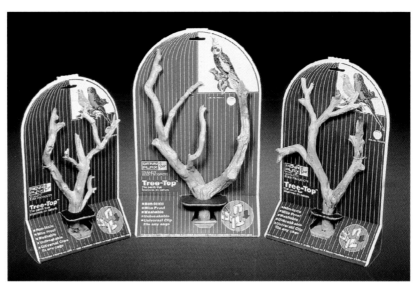

Examples of foods parrots can enjoy with you are whole grain breakfast cereals and breads, pasta, rice and bean dishes, cooked egg casseroles, well-cooked bones, cooked shrimp, shellfish and fish, cooked and raw vegetables and fruits, yogurt, small portions of meats, nuts, whole grain crackers and dried fruits. Save "wet" foods for meal times, since wet foods should be discarded within an hour to prevent bacterial contamination. Choose drier foods to leave in the cage, such as seeds and pellets, dried fruits, unsalted pretzels, alfalfa cubes and nuts. Raw greens, peppers, carrots,

Darker greens and vegetables such as spinach, escarole and broccoli are higher in their vitamin content than lighter ones such as celery and lettuce.

peas and beans are usually safe to be left in the cage all day; these foods are rarely eaten once they wilt, and even then, they are not likely to be dangerous. The same applies to fresh whole items, such as grapes, cranberries or blueberries, and cherry tomatoes and peppers. Wetter and sweeter fruits, such as cut-up peaches or mangoes, may spoil if left in the cage all day. It is advisable to remove fruit pits and seeds (except for grapes, melons and squash relatives) since some may be toxic.

Continue offering foods that your bird rejects. Some birds eat certain foods only seasonally or periodically. My Timneh Grey Parrot, for example, may eat a full green pepper for several days in a row, then ignore peppers for months. There are periods when nothing but nuts will be consumed, but then fruits and greens will be favored over them. My Red-bellied Parrot, on the other hand, samples everything daily and never seems to crave too much of any one thing. While we all love to see birds eating like my Red-bellied, it is important to realize that the pattern of food consumption varies among species and individuals within a species. My Timneh, for instance, may be eating appropriately for its species. Timnehs live in

If your pet parrot will spend the better part of the day away from its cage, be sure to offer it foods that it can nibble upon during this time.

Hand-feeding formulas supply baby parrots with all the necessary vitamins to grow into well-nourished birds.

humid areas where flocks travel looking for crops that are just ripe. Once they find them, they consume them and then move on to another area. Red-bellied Parrots live in arid areas where they may have to eat small morsels of whatever they find, without wasting much energy by being picky. So different birds may be programmed to eat in different ways.

Parrots are naturally suspicious of new foods, or foods presented in different ways, or even in different bowls. While this is not usually a problem with babies, some species, like Greys, may develop this attitude at a very young age. If a bird trusts you, you may demonstrate a good food by eating some. With older birds

Cuttlebone and mineral blocks provided in your pet's cage are an added source of minerals and calcium. These should be available to your bird at all times.

that have been kept on limited diets for a long time, change may come very slowly, but it is always possible. Patience and creativity will pay off.

You may try to change the ways in which food is presented. Some birds will not eat chopped fruits or vegetables, but they may devour the same items if presented clipped to toys or cage bars as if they were hanging from trees. Some will eat carrots or sweet potatoes only if they are cooked, others only if they are raw. Parrots may have other concerns regarding food: one of my parrots won't touch a piece of banana with her feet, but will eat it from my hand. I believe the fussy brat just doesn't want to mess up her own toes! Experiment creatively with your own birds.

Try to pay attention to vitamin A intake. Some birds develop deficiencies, and this deficiency could be serious. A parrot does not need to eat any one particular thing to stay healthy. If it won't take carrots, try broccoli, red peppers, dried papaya, sweet potatoes, winter squashes, or mangoes. As long as you see some vitamin A-rich item being consumed regularly, you don't need to worry.

Chewing and exploring objects are some of the ways in which healthy birds spend their time. Fresh, non-toxic tree branches make fine chewing materials to give to your birds.

With a well-balanced diet and the correct amount of vitamin supplement, your pet parrot will remain in excellent feather condition and good overall health.

Calcium deficiency is also possible, especially in growing babies and egg-laying female birds. Cuttlebone and mineral blocks always should be available. In addition, calcium-rich foods, such as kale, collard greens, broccoli, bones, shrimp shells and limited dairy products should be offered daily.

A sure way to get calcium and vitamin A into your birds is to bake little muffins loaded with these nutrients. My birds, not very fussy, are the only members of the family who appreciate my baking. I usually mix in the blender one small box of muesli cereal, one or two eggs *with shell*, a couple of carrots, raisins, a tablespoon of oil or

peanut butter, and some milk or fruit juice, as needed for consistency. Then I place the mixture in a muffin pan and bake it until done. There is no need to use baking soda or powder (too much sodium can be harmful and your birds won't care about the muffins being flat).

Birds that eat a good diet don't need vitamin and mineral supplements. In fact, because some pellets are heavily supplemented, further addition of vitamins may lead to toxicity. Most birds, however, do not consume a varied diet and therefore vitamin supplements available from your local pet store may be required.

Some vets and breeders believe that pelleted diets are the only way to assure proper intake because a mixture of seed and pellets allows the bird to pick its favorite items. Still others believe that exclusively pelleted diets promote feather plucking due to boredom, and may contribute to health problems in the long term. I rather err on the side of the bird by offering choices and fun through varied foods. There are only so many ways in which a bird can entertain itself in a cage. Looking

forward to feedings and variety enriches its life and well being, if nothing else through fun. How would you like to eat a perfectly balanced chow day after day?

If you ever need to feed something out of a bag, due to illness, travel, or other personal reasons, the best choice is a good seed, dried fruit and pellet mixture. These mixtures are available from your local pet store and usually contain at least sunflower, safflower, millet, oats, dried corn, peas, beans, crumbs or pellets, peanuts, dried chili peppers and nuts. Some better ones also contain nuts and pieces of dried fruits such as raisins, berries, papaya and pineapple. The main complaint about these diets is waste. No parrot will eat every item in the mix. You can minimize waste by feeding a fixed amount that would force the bird to eat more than just one or two items. However, you should always have in the cage some foods that the bird will accept, and no matter how much is left, you should discard it and replace it with fresh, clean food each day. Because birds may lose weight very quickly, no bird should be put on a restrictive diet unless under veterinary instructions and supervision.

Most parrots, even cockatiels, will pick through their food for their favorite items. Much food is wasted in this manner, either by being cast out of the dish and left on the floor of the cage, or thrown completely from the cage.

ALONG THE WAY

SOCIALIZATION AND TRAINING

I discuss socialization and training together because they are closely related. Some people like to train their parrots to do special tricks, such as riding a scooter. This book won't get into that type of training. It will focus strictly on training necessary to have a good, well-adjusted pet, which may include a few tricks, generally selected by your parrot.

The most basic routine you need to learn is to pick up your parrot. Always say something like "up" when you do it, and then really do it. *Be gentle but firm.* This is the key with all parrots, much like with young children. While they may challenge your authority, they need *you* to stay in control. Gently place one finger (or two, or the side of your hand, depending on the bird's size) at the top of the legs, pushing up on

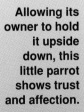

Allowing its owner to hold it upside down, this little parrot shows trust and affection.

the belly. Provide just enough pressure so the bird has to step up or lose balance. Eventually, when you say "up," your bird should raise a foot and get ready.

Always use this command to regain control of your bird in a biting situation. *Never, ever, strike a bird, no matter how gently.* Yelling and scaring a parrot may permanently damage your relationship while getting no benefit whatsoever. Accept the fact that a parrot will challenge your dominant status in the flock every now and then. Don't play in and start a mind game with the bird. Remember it's just a bird! You *are* the dominant member of the flock. If your bird challenges your status, calmly use the "up" command, give the bird a firm, hard look, place it in the cage and withdraw attention for a moment. While the cage should not be used as punishment, because you want your pet to be happy there, it is the only place where you should leave the bird unsupervised. If you have a good relationship with your parrot, the bird will react to your leaving the room or withdrawing attention, rather than to going back in the cage.

Because each bird is different, you should experiment different approaches with your own pet. One of my parrots does not respond to

scolding when she bites, but she readily responds to "guilt trips." If I softly say "No, be gentle, you are hurting me," she immediately sweetens up, whereas saying "No! Bad bird!" has no effect.

There are a few other lessons that are worth giving to your bird as early as possible. These lessons are geared to handling that

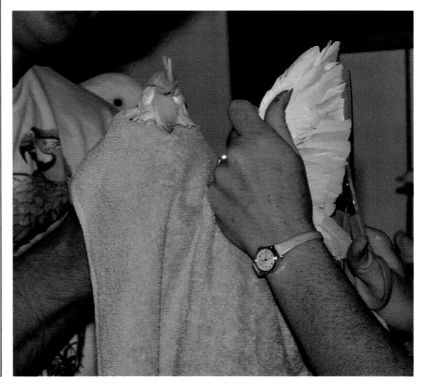

towel. If they are introduced to this early, at a quiet time of day such as before bedtime, most parrots learn to enjoy it. Then, when it becomes necessary to wrap your pet for wing clipping or physical examination, the parrot won't get very upset. Simply put a towel of appropriate size on a counter, gently place your baby on it and fold the ends over it. Then pick up your bundle and do whatever pleases your bird, such as singing, tickling, cuddling, talking softly or rocking gently.

may be necessary to provide proper care later on.

I like to get my birds used to being wrapped in a

Another useful routine is a belly-up roll. Vets often need to get birds in this position for grooming and examination. The first time

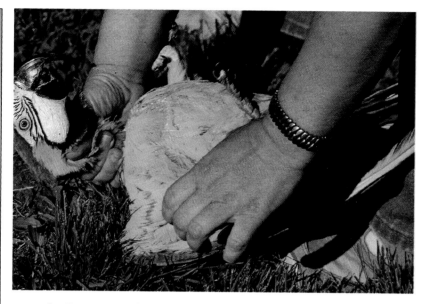

Some parrots do not like to be rolled over on their back. This action must be introduced to the bird at a very young age.

you do this, your baby is likely to get nervous and flap its wings. Always be very gentle and progress as slowly as your bird allows you. Some birds like to roll on their backs and even scare their owners by sleeping in that position.

Baby parrots need soft surfaces to walk and rest upon.

Always be gentle with your bird and progress slowly. Fast movements frighten most birds.

Others find this position very threatening and feel very vulnerable, so be sensitive to your bird's mood. I gently hold the bird with one hand and cup its back with the other. I then start rolling the bird gently to one side saying something like "I'm gonna roll you." I keep it very brief and repeat it a couple of times a day, always saying the same. Eventually, the bird knows what's coming when it hears the phrase. Usually, that ends the

wings handled. Remember that some birds may never like this; respect their preference. Still, a gentle, brief attempt regularly, will reduce stress at wing clipping time or vet visits.

Some parrot experts consider that patting the back of a parrot is a form of abuse, even if the bird learns to tolerate it. It is true that parrots are naturally protective of their back, which in the wild is rarely touched except during an attack by a predator. However, hand-fed parrots are usually very trusting of their owners. To say that touching their back will always cause them stress is an over generalization. My African Grey, for example, has her own way of communicating fear to me. When she spots a predator in the sky, she

anxiety, and at this point I can start adding something such as "tickle your belly" or "tickle your feet."

While the towel wrap is best introduced at a quiet time, it is best to do the belly-up roll at a playful time. It is a good idea to get really silly with your birds for a while each day. They become less anxious about loud vocalizations and rougher movements by associating them with play. They'll learn that no matter how puppy-like your game gets, you can remain gentle and sensitive to their size.

I also recommend getting birds used to having their back stroked and their

Many parrots will often produce a dropping from the same perch. You can learn your parrot's favorite places by careful observation, and then act upon these by placing a sheet of newspaper below the spots outside of the cage.

Parrots that are used to having some sort of roof over their heads will be a bit leery of an open sky when they are placed outside in an open yard.

There are tell-tale signs of a parrot's aggressiveness, such as this cockatoo with its feathers fluffed and crest raised, that one should beware of.

freezes, fixes her eyes on me and slowly bats her eyelids. When I respond by coming to her, she waits until I am a few inches away, then dives quickly under my chin, sticks her head under my collar and "wants" to be covered and held. I say this because I can actually feel her breathing and heartbeat slowing down as I pet her and talk to her for a while, until she emerges reassured. Although she is loving with everyone in the family, she makes it clear by turning and groaning that she doesn't want anyone else touching her back. We respect this. We humans, however, have a tendency to treat our pets as babies, often forgetting that they have different tendencies and preferences, and force inappropriate contact on them. Always be respectful of your bird's individuality and try to reinforce behaviors that will make your life together easier without antagonizing your pet.

TOILET TRAINING

Another behavior that is desirable for parrots is toilet training. It is important to know what

this means when applied to a bird. First, not every bird is trainable in this respect.

Cockatoos enjoy being cuddled and handled. In general, they do not feel safe if held out on your arm away from your body.

Toilet training of parrots is relatively easy with patience and good observational skills. By repeating the command, while holding the bird over a chosen area when a dropping is anticipated, most birds learn to associate this command with the action and deliver on request. (Important: *Never flush a toilet while a bird is nearby. An unexpected jump or fall at the wrong time could end in disaster.*)

Second, it is unreasonable to expect never to have "an accident." Third, we should respect each bird's individual preferences and tendencies. In a way, this is a mutual training experience. You should observe your bird, learn about its likes and dislikes, and then try to work out a communication system that serves you both. Rather than giving a recommendation on how to toilet train a bird, I'll give a few real examples:

1. My Quaker Parakeet never dropped on me. There was no teaching or training involved, except for observation and sensitivity to her needs. Every twenty

Parrots that will be spending a better part of the day on a stand or perch can have a sheet of newspaper placed below them to catch their droppings.

minutes or so of holding her, I would place her on her cage top, where she would produce a dropping; I would then pick her up again. Because this was over thirty years ago and, as a child, I was told this type of training was totally impossible, I thought life could keep delivering one happy coincidence after another.

2. Before my Timneh Grey was even fully feathered, I noticed she would always produce a dropping as soon as I took her out of her cage. It was as if she had been holding the dropping. I started

placing her on a newspaper sheet immediately after getting her out and saying "poopy" every time she dropped. Very soon, she

Some parrots can be trained to drop on command prior to letting them out of their cage. However, accidents do occur.

Always remember that a parrot is not a human and it cannot always control when or where it produces a dropping.

Pet stores will carry a wide range of special stands that you may keep your pet on while it is out of its cage.

learned to make a dropping whenever I said "go poopy," which I do every time I take her out of the cage, and every twenty minutes thereafter, only if I'm holding her. Sometimes she even says "poopy" or "uh, oh..." when she has to go. Because she does hate dropping in her cage, I place a litter pan lined with newspaper under the cage's open door while she plays on top of it. Whenever she needs to, she perches on top of the door and drops right in the pan. This behavior was never taught; in fact, I would much prefer that she liked to drop in her cage, which gets

Some birds will only produce droppings from certain perches in their cage. Be considerate to your pet's needs and place it back into its cage so that it may take care of its business.

cleaned daily anyway. Since we all work full time or go to school, often she has no choice, but the size of her droppings in the cage shows how much she hates having to do it.

3. My Red-bellied Parrot seems to prefer dropping from a certain perch in his cage and even while playing on top of the cage he often goes to that same corner to drop. He always gets a warm, soft meal for breakfast, which he eats out of a bowl on a counter. When he is done, I clean his beak and place him on a sheet of newspaper on the floor, and say "poopy." He soon learned what this meant, and now he promptly produces his big morning dropping on request. I then pick him up, tell him what a good boy he is (sometimes my Timneh beats me to it) and tickle him. Then he goes about his day, dropping as he pleases in his cage. I only use the command again if I intend to hold him for a while and want to feel "safe."

4. One of my male cockatiels liked to perch on his cage top pen. Whenever he got the urge, he descended, walked to the edge of the cage, turned around to point his tail towards the outside, and

Some birds will relieve themselves wherever nature calls. This is something that cannot be helped and one must clean up the mess and forget it.

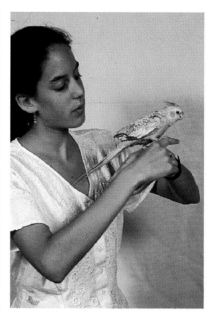

Try not to manipulate your pet's every dropping. There should be some places, such as outdoors, where your pet is allowed to drop without having you run under it to clean up immediately.

produced a dropping, then returned to his perch. Because he was a hand-tame shy bird, who didn't like to ride on people's shoulders, placing a newspaper beside the cage provided all the convenience of a toilet trained bird. Another male cockatiel, however, relieved himself wherever nature called. Because he liked to ride on people, we would wait to pick him up until just after he evacuated and put him back on his perch a short while later.

Some people think that a parrot may become dependent on a verbal command and refuse to defecate unless the command is given. I don't believe this is true, as long as rigidity is avoided. **Never scold a bird for dropping.** Holding droppings for too

long may be harmful to a bird's health. Scolding and inflexible schedules may cause discomfort, whether they involve a verbal command or not. For example, a parrot that *always* has to defecate on newspaper may have trouble doing it from a perch. One that is *always* held over the toilet to drop, may not want to do it anywhere else. The key to preventing these compulsions is to avoid any *always*. There is no need to manipulate your pet's every dropping. The goal is not to be hit by one! Even if you do get hit once in a while, don't make a big deal out of it. Clean up and forget about it, much like you would do if a toddler had an accident.

Certain toys may hold hidden dangers.
Your birds should only be permitted to
play with such items when under your
supervision.

TOYS

Most parrots like to play with toys. In general, toys may be grouped in four categories:

• **Preening toys:** These toys are geared to satisfy a parrot's need to preen a peer's feathers. If this need is not fulfilled, parrots may resort to overpreening, damaging or plucking their own feathers. These toys usually have pieces of fabric, leather and rope. All parrots should have at least one toy of this type. Since these toys are porous, hang them from the side or top of the cage near a perch or a swing, to avoid soiling with droppings. Cotton rope and fabrics, jute, sisal and untanned leather strips with knots are considered generally safe. However, some parrots ingest fibers, which could lead to crop impaction and blockages.

Always observe your bird's behavior with a new toy. If you see actual ingestion of material, remove the toy. Also, frayed fibers of sufficient length may wrap around toes cutting off circulation. Keep all fibers short.

• **Chewing toys:** All parrots need to chew and tear up materials. Many toys are marketed for durability and labeled "indestructible." While these toys may provide other types of entertainment, they won't satisfy the need to chew and tear. Depending on your parrot's size and type, you need to find toys that challenge this skill and provide relief. A paper towel to rip and a few small sticks or twigs may be all a budgie can handle. An empty toilet paper roll may be enough for a cockatiel. A macaw may need large

These baby Amazon parrots enjoy the interaction and exercise provided by a playpen.

chunks of hard woods, black walnuts, Brazil and hickory nuts. Well-cooked bones may also provide chewing satisfaction. Some rubber and nylon toys are made of non-toxic, safe materials intended for chewing.

• **Hard toys:** These include acrylics, metals and generally durable toys that can be manipulated and examined with beaks and feet. Some good ones are acrylic boxes for treats, rattles and plastic chains. While some children's toys may be appropriate for parrots, some of these toys may shatter under the power of a strong beak and cause injury. Always examine toys very carefully and supervise play with new toys.

• **Sounding toys:** Most parrots enjoy bells, rattles and music boxes. Bells should be of appropriate material, size and strength, or they may trap and injure beaks. Select only lead free bells. A pleasant sound is an advantage, since the whole family will be hearing it. Music boxes designed for parrots are commercially available. Other music boxes may cause injury.

A new toy in your bird's cage may be left un-touched for a few days until it becomes accustomed to it. Do not place a new toy near your bird's feed dish because, if frightened, your pet may not eat.

You can provide a lot of interesting homemade toys that are safe, inexpensive and just as likely to please your bird as the most expensive gadgets you will find. Stuffing old socks with nuts, wood and other small objects and tying them to playpen perches can provide hours of fun. I don't use these in the cages where my birds play without supervision because I fear the socks may unravel and strangle toes, or worse.

Nuts provide lots of entertainment. Smaller birds may need these partially cracked. Pecan nuts are softer than walnuts, but more slippery; press them in the middle until they get a few cracks. Very small birds may enjoy peanuts in the shell or pumpkin seeds.

Corks wrapped in a paper napkin or towel amuse many birds. Supervise to make sure your bird won't ingest the cork. Metal bottle caps, pieces of packing boxes, brown bags filled with popcorn and paper towel tubes stuffed with nuts, can entertain your bird while you are away. Always

give them play foods and special toys when you will be gone longer than usual.

GAMES

When you play games that capture your pet's interest, you are more likely to have fun teaching tricks. The most important factor in learning is motivation. For most parrots, shared fun is a stronger reward than food. To recognize what causes your bird to have fun will be invaluable, not only for teaching tricks and games, but for reinforcing desirable behaviors and for discouraging negative ones.

Once I got silly with a baby parrot, mouthing her foot while saying "I'm

You may, at times, find that your pet parrot wishes to play a game with you. Perhaps it will try to steal your money while you are figuring out your bills!

gonna eat your foot." To my total surprise, a few days later this baby stuck her foot in my mouth saying "eat your foot." Almost four years later, this is still one of our favorite games. When she starts it, I get very theatrical telling her how delicious her foot is. She repeats the game alternating feet for as long as I'm willing to play. If I say "gimme your foot," she lifts up her leg without hesitation.

By following your parrot's lead in games, you will end up with a "trick trained" bird that has been active in designing its own tricks. This beats pre-packaged trick training, such as those involving commercial props. Remember that your bird is a flock member, not a clown. You should laugh *with* your pet, rather than *at* your pet. It's more challenging to try to discover your bird's nature than to work at teaching meaningless routines.

Reserve this type of training energy to teach the rules you need to live happily with your bird.

BITING AND SCREAMING

These are the behaviors that cause the most problems with pet birds. Biting is a normal bird behavior that is used to control other members of its flock. Most species of parrots have clear ways of signaling aggression prior to resorting to biting. This results in fewer injuries.

Play-pens, such as this one, can provide birds with a change in surroundings. They are helpful to decrease territorial aggression around the cage.

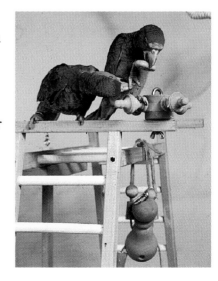

While it is helpful to recognize these warning signals and to respect them, in your relationship with your parrot you will always need to maintain a higher pecking order to avoid problems. Your parrot is likely to challenge this hierarchy periodically, but it should be easy to maintain dominance by following a few rules.

Because dominant birds tend to get the higher perches, it is recommended that your bird's cage and perches remain lower than "yours." While you are "perched" on the floor, your parrot relates to your head as your person, and to your body as your perch. This is one of the reasons why a parrot should not be allowed to perch on shoulders. Another reason is that (except for budgies

or cockatiels) beaks may cause serious injury to a face. Even birds that have never bit before may do it without warning.

Babies may start biting very early, usually as a way of begging for food or

Some parrots, such as the cockatoo, are known to be quite noisy.

Most parrots go through a period where they begin to feel independent or become a little nippy. If your pet nips or refuses to step up on your hand, a firm command should be given immediately and briefly, or else your pet may not associate it with the action.

Pet parrots will become possessive of certain toys. To avoid this try changing the toys in your pet's cage from time to time.

exploring your fingers. You may allow gentle mouthing of your fingers. Your baby's tongue is very sensitive and it is used to explore textures and shapes. If your bird starts applying pressure on you, quickly jerk the hand on which the baby is perched and say "No." This jerk has to be appropriate to the bird's size. It's always a good idea to start with a gentle jerk, because the first time you do it, it's likely to startle the bird much more than in the future.

If you scream, make faces, shake and curse when a parrot bites, you may very well be asking for more. This is called *drama reward*. If your bird finds your behavior interesting, biting again is your bird's way of saying "encore!" to your performance. You need to produce an *immediate unwanted response*. This response should not damage the trust that your bird has placed in you. For this reason, the bird should feel displeased but never threatened. No matter how much your pet disappoints you, scaring or hitting a bird should never be part of your response. If you can't control your responses, you should consider finding another home for your bird.

A pet parrot will usually test the toughness of a structure with its beak before it steps up onto this. Do not be frightened by this and try to pull away because you may cause the bird to clamp on harder and inflict a nasty bite.

Always be careful with your bird when confronted with strangers. When someone asks you if your bird bites, say "yes." Even if your bird never bit anybody before, parrots lack the predictability of a well-trained dog. Almost any parrot will respond differently to different people. You must minimize handling by strangers for your pet's safety as well as your guests'. I know of a bird that was killed when a surprised stranger shook his hand too hard in response to a bite, smashing the parrot against a tile floor. It's very hard to get over such a tragedy.

Many birds need to reach for a hand or a finger with their beak before they step on it. Withdrawing the hand in fear may be taken as teasing and it can result in a biting habit. Once you

Birds can display attitudes which can either be construed as aggressive behavior or playful behavior.

Parrots will become territorial of their cage or their play area if permitted to spend a great deal of time there. To avoid this, have several areas designated in the house where your parrot will be able to play.

say "up," you must be determined to pick up your bird. It is your *command*, not an open invitation.

If you are afraid of bites, get a very small bird, or one with an established docile nature. Almost all birds periodically go through stages of some biting and your fear may perpetuate the problem. Some parrots have hormonal swings when they mature and need to be handled differently for a few months each year. Others have certain times during the day when they use more aggression. Learn to "read" your bird and avoid problems by recognizing moods.

Another situation that may result in biting is cage bonding. If a parrot spends all the time in or on a cage, it may become very protective of this territory. It is recommended to have several areas in the house

where your parrot can spend some time daily. I have a hanging perch in the bathtub, so I can spend more morning time with my bird. This provides feather misting, play, shared grooming time and time away from the cage. It is also good to have at least one portable perch that can be taken around to different rooms. Wooden sweater racks on cafeteria trays make great inexpensive pens for small parrots. Hanging a few toys and a food cup is all you need to complete the transformation.

Some parrots, much like young children, may be over stimulated in play to a point where they lose self-restraint. This is quite common with Amazons. If you notice your pet getting too excited, let it work out its energy with a piece of wood, rubber or rope.

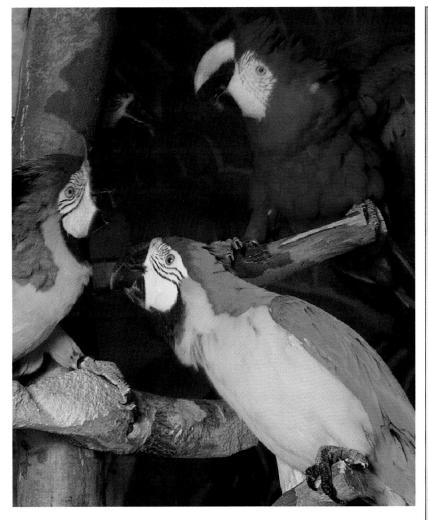

One pet parrot can make quite a bit of noise, but several together can be unbearable.

Pupil flashing can be a warning sign, but it can also signal positive excitement or attention. Tail flashing is usually a precursor to attack. Rubbing the beak against a perch while there is no food on it, or swinging the head from side to side may signal trouble as well. If there is no need to approach your bird at these times, don't. It may save both of you a negative interaction.

Screaming can be very problematic, both for your family and for your neighbors. It is important to differentiate "problem" screaming from normal vocalizations. Depending on the species of parrot, loud vocalizations may be completely unavoidable. Most parrots vocalize loudly during a couple of daily periods, usually in the morning and evening. "Loudly" is a relative term that differs for each

A screaming bird should not be rewarded by having you come to it to yell back or remove it for play. This will only reinforce the act. Instead, wait until the bird quiets down, and then take it out for play or go to its cage and talk quietly.

species, and even individuals. This type of vocalization is intrinsically rewarding to the bird. Interfering with this behavior by, for example, distracting the bird, may reinforce and prolong the behavior if the parrot enjoys the distraction.

Sometimes parrots scream to get attention or to be taken out of their cage. This type of screaming can be curbed by ignoring it and by rewarding appropriate behavior. If you simply ignore the parrot, you won't get results; in fact, the problem may get worse. Consistently take your parrot out at the times your bird is accustomed to expect it. Don't wait until your pet reminds you with screams. Be attentive to your bird and provide

Two parrots kept together will often have small spats in which they can become very vocal.

intermittent attention during quiet times or when it calls in an appropriate manner. If you are busy and your pet calls "Hello... I love you..." go ahead and spoil it a little. Nobody should mind this kind of manipulation too much.

Some parrots learn to fake a crisis in the following way. The first time they fear to be caught in a toy, they scream, which immediately brings the whole family running. Bingo! Let's try it again... Because you can't ignore your bird's screams unless you are totally sure nothing is wrong, in many cases you will have to check your pet, even if you suspect this type of trick. However, be alert and aware of this and make the experience as neutral as possible.

Baby parrots need to feel secure. This can be achieved by keeping them in the proper environment, or with other baby birds.

SECURITY AND FLEXIBILITY

Fostering a sense of security by providing a predictable environment is essential. However, you also want your parrot to be able to cope with change. To balance adaptability and predictability you must expose your pet to diverse experiences and flexible routines. One way of walking this fine line is to try to make each unusual experience an exciting one for your pet. For example, if you usually have dinner with your bird, on the days you don't, cook its favorite meal. Feed it in the cage just as you are leaving, and throw in a special toy or an entertaining "dessert." If you take your bird to a picnic, bring special treats. Save your pet's favorite fruits to distract it during a car trip in a carrier.

At least once a month, starting at a very young age, change something in your parrot's cage. Rearrange perches, replace toys, or add a new swinging rope. Make the change noticeable, but not too drastic. This will help

Your pet parrot must learn to be flexible to your needs. Very often birds become dependent on a specific schedule that when deviated from they become thrown out of their element. Change your bird's surroundings from time to time and rearrange the cage to avoid such happenings.

your parrot accept novelty, rather than becoming too dependent on a given arrangement for comfort and security. This is particularly important for African Greys, who can become extremely anxious about any change in their environment if not accustomed to it.

Before you place a new toy in the cage, test the bird's reaction to it. Occasionally, the toy you thought your pet would love will cause panic. Leave it within view of your bird, a few feet from the cage, for a few days. You may play with the toy in front of your bird to gradually reduce anxiety. Never rush this process. No matter how unfounded it seems, this fear is a serious matter to your pet.

Risking ridicule, I'll share with you something I do to reassure my birds. Every time I leave the house or take them somewhere, I tell them what will happen. "I have to go, you have to stay in your cage, I'll be back for supper" or "We are going to go in the car, we'll go see Pat" are too complex statements for me to believe that my parrots understand them. However, they quiet down and listen,

Comfort your pet when it becomes frightened or seems nervous. This will strengthen the bond between you and your pet.

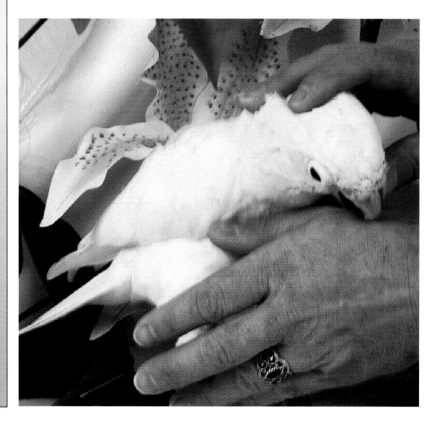

Always make sure you are welcome with your pet on visits before arriving.

pupils flashing with attention, and often they appear reassured. While I refuse to even speculate any further about this, I see no harm in doing it, if it helps.

Short vacations with your bird can be enjoyable. They can also teach your pet that it's possible to have fun away from home. While some hotels will allow a caged bird or two, it is usually easier to share a vacation at a rental location.

Taking your bird to visit family and friends is another way of fostering flexibility. Since not every household would welcome a parrot, always get permission in advance. In addition, if unfamiliar children, cats or dogs will be present, it's best to not bring your parrot.

Parrots can learn to mimic speech from a very early age. Begin by repeating the same word or phrase over and over from the very first day you bring your pet home.

TALKING

The best way to teach a bird to talk is by talking. Chat with your bird in the same way you would chat with a young child. Name objects that are interesting to your bird, such as foods, familiar pets, people and toys. Say the same thing for the same situation. For example, if you always say "Wanna come out?" when you are about to take your pet out of its cage, the bird is likely to associate it with the situation and eventually use it to request to come out.

Singing, whistling and dancing are enjoyed by most birds. While some parrots never learn to talk, they can communicate excitement and affection in other ways. Observe and even imitate your parrot to

The more birds that are housed together in a cage, the more feed and cleaning they will require.

discover what elicits the most interest.

Tapes marketed to teach birds to talk are of limited value and can be annoying to intelligent birds. While there is nothing wrong with using them for short periods, leaving continuous tapes on while you go to work or school is inconsiderate.

TIME SAVING TIPS

Parrots demand a lot of care for many years of our lives. It is important to pace ourselves for a long-term commitment. By being practical, disciplined and organized you are less likely to feel that your birds have become a heavy burden. These are some of the things you may find helpful, particularly if you have a working family.

All parrots have the ability to learn to mimic speech, however, the degree to which they do varies among individual birds.

• **Cage cleaning:** If you work, clean the cage thoroughly on one of your days off and line the tray with enough layers of newspaper to last the week. Every morning or evening simply remove a layer of newspaper and replace all water and food dishes. Also clean any droppings or food spills that might have landed on perches, toys or cage bars. If your cage is an odd size, pre-cut a supply of paper liners once a week.

• **Cage area cleaning:** If possible, choose a washable non-porous floor, such as tile or linoleum, for the cage. If you must place the cage on carpet, you may glue linoleum to a large piece of wood and use it as a base for the cage. A rechargeable hand vacuum cleaner placed near the cage is extremely helpful. A little hand broom and dusting pan set is handy too. Keep a box of facial tissue nearby to wipe off droppings and minor spills that don't grant wasting a paper towel. If your bird perches on the cage door while spending time out, a cat

You may prepare a quantity of fresh produce for your pet parrot that will last for a few days in the refrigerator.

litter pan lined with newspapers placed under the door may be helpful to catch debris. Feed the messiest foods (such as mashed beets) outdoors or while on the shower perch. Most standard perches and play pens have shallow pans; replacing them with deeper ones helps catch more debris. Placing crocks in the center of the pens helps too.

• **Fresh produce preparation:** If you shop on your days off, trim and wash vegetables and fruits as soon as you get home. Place them in closed plastic bags in the refrigerator. You can get some out each morning, ready to serve. At dinner time, separate some salad for your bird prior to adding dressing, or some cooked vegetables prior to adding any butter or margarine.

Meal sharing with your parrot makes the most of little time.

All birds enjoy much the same foods as we do.

• **Meal sharing:** Almost any meal may be shared with birds, at least partially, particularly if you are health conscious. However, for the few occasions when a meal may be totally unsuitable, there are several easy and fast dinners you may prepare for your pet. Microwave a few frozen mixed vegetables and serve them with sprinkled grain cereal or small pieces of whole grain bread. Freeze a few small portions of pasta or bean

Many types of shower perches are commercially available. Showering with your bird is a practical way of extending your "quality time" together.

stews and heat them up as needed. Warm up a jar of a baby food dinner. Scramble an egg with frozen vegetables or chopped apples and raisins in the microwave. The possibilities are endless.

• **Making the most of little time:** If you live a busy life, it's easy to add a little quality time with your pet by sharing your shower. This is enjoyable for most birds and helps with bonding. There are many commercially available shower perches. You may have to be creative in figuring out how to adapt your particular shower for a parrot. If you shower in a bathtub or a large stall, you may be able to hang a swing from the ceiling or from the curtain rod and a nail on the wall. Add a few non-porous toys, such as acrylic and metal gadgets. If you sing in the shower, your pet is sure to have a ball.

EPILOGUE

—Every day new discoveries are made about parrots' needs and their proper care in captivity. Dietary recommendations are revised, new products are developed, diseases are better understood and their treatments improve. Continue to seek information and knowledge that will benefit your bird. Join a bird club, subscribe to a

We learn to provide proper care for our parrots through studies and experiments.

magazine, read related books. This will help you, in a real although limited way. You must remember that each parrot is a unique individual. Careful observation, respect and responsible concern will remain your best tools. The support of publications and other people's experiences will help you to provide better care. Two things that your parrot will always need the most of, are your love and attention.

Knowing the personality of your parrot will help you to know when something is amiss.

ABOUT THE AUTHOR

Delia Berlin completed her undergraduate education in Argentina and holds MS and MA degrees from The University of Connecticut. She obtained her first parrot as a young child and since then, she has had experience with South American, Australian and African bird species. She is newsletter editor for the Connecticut Association for Aviculture and her articles have been published in American Cage Bird Magazine, Parrot World and The AFA Watchbird. Currently, Ms. Berlin is an administrator for a community-technical college, and lives in Connecticut with her husband, David, her daughter, Ana, her Timneh African Grey, Eureka and her Red-bellied Parrot, Biko.

Photo of author with her Red-bellied parrot, "Biko."

Baby Blue and Gold Macaw.

INDEX

Page numbers in **boldface** refer to illustrations.

Accident prevention, 66
Accommodation, **27**
Active, 25 **25**, **45**
Affection, **7**, **39**, **42**, **86**
African Grey Parrot, 34, **34**, **58**, **93**
Aggressive, **16**, **17**, **92**, **108**
Aligned legs, **48**
Amazon, **27**, 36
—Blue-fronted, 36
—Double Yellow-headed, 36
—Hispanolian, **63**
—Lilac-crowned, 36
—Spectacled, 36
—White-fronted, 36
—Yellow-naped, 36
Aratinga, 32
Attention, 16, **39**, 63
Attractiveness, 26
Baby, 22
Bald spots, **46**
Barred Parakeet, **31**
Baths, **75**
Beak care, **72**, 73, **73**
Beak overgrowth, 73
Belly-up roll, 90
Bird carrier, 54, **52**, **55**
Bird clubs, 48
Biting, 17, 104–109, **106**, **107**
Blood feather, **68**, 71
Blood loss, 71
Blue and Gold Macaw, **71**, **121**
Boarding cage, 56
Body contact, 60
Brown-headed Parrot, 33
Budgerigar, **28**
Budgies, 27
Cage, 49

—Bar spacing, 50
—Bar strength, 50
—Casters, 52
—Floor grate, 51
—Heavy bowls, 53
—Large swing door, 51
—Location, **16**
—Natural perches, 53
—Playpen top, 52
—Shape, 49, **50**
—Size, **10**, 50
—Sliding tray, 50
—Swing-out feeders, 52
—Swings, 54
Cage area cleaning, 115
Calcium, 83, **83**
Cape Parrot, 33
Captive conditions, 12
Cere, 27
Chewing, 73, **82**
Closed band, 19, **19**
Cockatiel, **24**, **26**, 29, **29**, 85
Cockatoo, 37, **93**, **105**
Comfortable, 62
Commands, 68, 87, **88**, **105**
Contact, **12**
Conure, 31, **32**
Cost, 27
Cuddling, 26, **49**, 93
Cuttlebone, 83, **83**
Diets, 76
Disease, **60**, 65
Displacement behavior, 10
Domestic, 18, 19, **19**
Dropping, 43, **45**, **94**, **95**, **96**
Eating, 60
Eclectus, 38, **38**, **43**
Exercise, **50**

Exposure to other birds, 41
Eyes, 47
Feather dust, 37
Feather plucking, 35, 84
Feeding routines, 61
Flexibility, 15, **62**, 63, 111–113
Flexible, **111**
Flying ability, 73
Food, 15, 56
—Fresh, 15, 78
—Preparation time, 15
—Calcium rich, 83
—New, 83
—People, **77**
—Soft, 61, **77**
—Wet, 80
Fruit trees, 79
Fruits, **54**, **79**
Games, **89**, 103, **104**
Gnaw, **52**
Goffin's Cockatoo, **49**
Good listening, 60
Greens, 78, **80**
Hand-fed, **4**, 10, 14, 18, 19, **22**, 24, **29**
Household plants, **69**
Identification, 19, **21**
Illness, **60**
Immune system, **65**
Imported, **18**, 19
Imprinting, **15**, 18, **18**
Indian Ringneck Parakeet, 34, **34**
Intelligence, 10
Jardine Parrot, 33
Legs, 47
Life-long bonds, 15
Life-spans, 12
Lories, 32, **32**
Lovebirds, 30, **30**
Macaws, **25**, 37, **37**, **79**
Meal sharing, 117, **116**
Mexican Red-headed Amazon, **44**
Meyer's Parrot, 33
Mimic, **26**, **28**, **114**, **115**

Mineral blocks, 83, **83**
Mis-aligned beak, **48**
Missing toes, 47
Molting, 46, 70
Moluccan Cockatoo, **27**
Monk Parakeet, 31, **31**
Nail trimming, 70, **72**, **73**
Nanday Conure, **56**
Natural branches, **52**
Nervous, 76, **112**
Night light, 57
Noise, 16, 27, **109**
Nostrils, 47
Nutrition, 76, **76**
Nuts, **79**, 81
"One person bird", **36**, **59**, 63
Open band, 19, **19**
Outdoor cage, 75
Outdoor play, 73
Parent-raised, 18, 19
Parrotlets, 31
Patience, **27**
Perches, **67**, 72
Personality, **23**, **24**
Pet-sitting, 15
Picinics, **75**
Pionus Parrot, 36, **36**
—Blue-headed, 37
—Bronze-winged, 37
—Maximilian, 37
—White-capped, 37
Play, 16, **47**
Playful, **33**
Playpen, 51, 56, **101**, **104**
Poicephalus, 33
Portable home, 76
Predators, 74, **74**
Preening, 43, 67
Primary feathers, 69
Proventricular Dilation Syndrome, 64
Psitacula, 34
Psittacine beak and feather disease, 46, 64
Pyrrhura, 32
Quaker, 31

Quarantine, 64–66, **64**
Quiet rest, 63
Red-bellied Parrot, 33
Red-masked Conure, **32**
Resting place, 66
Routine, 63
Rules, 17, **17**
Safe surroundings, 74
Salmon-crested Cockatoo, **39**
Screaming, 104–110, **110**
Secondary feathers, 70
Security, **12**, 24, 111–113
Seed diet, 77
Senegal Parrot, 33, **33**
Sexually dimorphic, 38
Short trips, **75**
Shower perch, 118, **118**
Size, 24
Sleep, 45, **47**
Social bonding, 79
Social stimulation, **103**
Socialization, 35, 86
Startled, 74
Stress, **41**
Styptic powder, 71
Sun Conure, **25**, **48**
Supervise, **68**
Swing door, **50**
Talk, 25, **33**, **34**, 114
Territorial, **108**, 104
Toenail care, 72

Toilet Training, 15, 93–98, **93**
Towel wrapping, **88**, 89
Toxic substances, 68, **69**
Toys, **10**, **53**, 55, **55**, 60, **61**, 98, **99**, **105**
—Chewing, 100
—Hanging, **61**
—Hard, 101
—Homemade, 102, **102**
—Household, **56**
—New, 100
—Preening, 100, **100**
—Sounding, 101
Training, 86
Tree branches, **82**
Tricks, 86
Trip home, 58
Trust, **20**, **86**
Umbrella Cockatoo, **42**
Understanding, **27**
Varied perches, **10**, **67**, 72
Vegetables, **54**, **79**, **80**
Vertical bars, **10**
Veterinarian, 48, 61
Vitamin supplement, **84**, 84, **81**
Vocal, **110**
Weaned, **57**
Weight loss, 46
Wild-caught, 18, 19
Wing clipping, **66**, 69, **70**, **74**
Wing span, **25**

H-1044
By Dr. A.E. Decoteau
128 pages. 37 black and white
photos, 97 full-color photos.

H-1079
By Dieter Hoppe
168 pages. Illustrated with
over 70 full-color photos.

KW-032
By Dr. Matthew M. Virends
and Dr. Herbert R. Axelrod
96 pages. 47 full-color
photos; 21 black and white
photos.

T-109
By Marshall Naigh
63 pages. Illustrated with
color photos throughout.

CO-028S
By Duke of Bedford
Contains 108 full-color
photos and 28 full-color
line drawings.

H-912
By Henry J. Bates and
Robert L. Busenbark
494 pages. 107 black and white
photos and 160 color photos.

SK-031
By Elaine Radford
64 pages. Contains over 50
full-color photos and
drawings.

PS-753
By Joseph M. Forshaw
584 pages. Approx. 300 large color plates
depicting close to 500 different parrots;
many line illustrations.

t.f.h.

1 T.F.H. Plaza
Neptune, NJ 07753

T.F.H. Publications offers the most comprehensive selection of books dealing with pet birds. A selection of significant titles is presented here; they and the many other works published by T.F.H. are available from your local pet shop, or write to us for a free catalog.

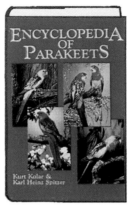

H-1094
By Kurt Kolar & Karl Heinz Spitzer
Contains many full color photos.

H-1109
544 pages. Contains over 300 full-color drawings and photos.

YF-113
By Martin Gabin
Illustrated with full-color photos throughout.

H-1088
By Wolfgang de Grahl
224 pages. 80 full-color and black and white photos.

TU-027
By William Wentworth
64 pages. 58 full-color photos.

H-1019
By Dr. E. Mulawka
349 pages. 152 full-color photos, 26 black and white.

AP-6450
By Dr. Jean Delacour
192 pages. 72 color photos, 27 black and white photos.

H-1055
By Klaus Bosch & Ursala Wedde
128 pages. Illustrated with full-color
photos and range maps.

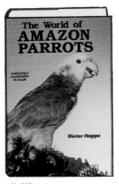

H-1093
By Dieter Hoppe
Hard cover, contains many full-
color photos.

CO-004S
By Dr. Matthew Virends
Illustrated throughout with
full-color photos.

TS-138
By Maja Muller-Bierl
144 pages. Contains 130
full-color photos.

PS-839
By Anne Ray Streeter
128 pages. 74 full-color
photos, 10 black and white
photos.

TT-007
By Jack C. Harris
Completely illustrated
throughout with full-color
photos.

KW-150
By Winifried Loeding
96 pages. 47 full-color
photos.

PS-746
By Dr. Gerald R. Allen
and Connie Allen
96 pages. Highly
illustrated with both
color and black and
white photos.

PS-801
By Dorothy Bulger
96 pages. Over 30 full-
color photos, 20 black
and white photos.

T-103
By Anmarie Barrie
Illustrated throughout
with full-color photos.

TS-159
By John Coborn
144 pages. Contains almost 200 full-color photos.

TS-107
By Carl Aschenborn
160 pages. Hardcover. Illustrated with many full-color photos throughout.

PS-797
By Howard Richmond
96 pages. Contains over 50 full-color photos, plus black and white photos.

TU-005
By John Coborn
Completely illustrated with full-color photos.

TS-140
By Nancy A. Reed
256 pages. 97 full-color photos unfold the spectrum of cockatiel color varieties.

TW-105
By Peter Small
256 pages. Completely illustrated with full color photos and drawings.

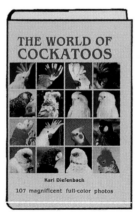

H-1072
By Karl Diefenbach
208 pages. Over 100 photos with more than 80 in full-color.

H-1052
By Robbie Harris
Fully illustrated with full-color photos.